THE ART
of the
Kitchen Garden

THE ART
of the
Kitchen Garden

JAN *and* MICHAEL GERTLEY

The Taunton Press

Taunton
BOOKS & VIDEOS
for fellow enthusiasts

Cover photo: Michael Gertley
Cover illustration: Jan Gertley

Printed in the United States of America
10 9 8 7 6 5 4 3 2 1

The Taunton Press, Inc.
63 South Main Street
PO Box 5506
Newtown, CT 06470-5506
e-mail: tp@taunton.com

Library of Congress Cataloging-in-Publication Data

Gertley, Jan.
    The art of the kitchen garden / Jan and Michael Gertley.
        p.   cm.
    ISBN 1-56158-180-1
    1. Vegetable gardening.   2. Gardens—Design.
    I. Gertley, Michael.   II. Title.
SB321.G375   1999   97-23710
    712'.6 — dc21   CIP

To all the gardeners who preceded us

∽ *Acknowledgments* ∽

*We would like to thank the following people
and establishments for their assistance in making
this book possible:*

To our friends and family
for giving us the gift of time.

To BJ and Rud for providing a helping hand
when it was needed most.

Our thanks also extend to the
Paleis Het Loo National Museum,
Apeldoorn, the Netherlands;
the Chateau de Villandry, Tours, France;
and to the Molbak family
for their friendship over the years
and for granting us permission to photograph their
beautiful nursery (pp. 115 and 117).

Lastly, a big thank you to Helen Albert,
Cherilyn DeVries, Tom McKenna, Carol Singer,
and the rest of the staff at The Taunton Press
for their support and participation
in this project.

Contents

*b*eyond the flower beds, tucked away at the far corner of our backyard, was a square of well-tilled soil reserved for our yearly plot of vegetables. Each spring, we arranged our garden in the same manner: successive, straight rows of leafy green vegetables, with small, compact varieties in the foreground and taller ones gradually ascending toward the rear. If any plants needed support, we quickly hammered together trellises with materials at hand. This frugal garden was very functional and productive. However, it lacked style.

Several years ago, while searching through a stack of garden books (one of our favorite pastimes), we were captivated by photographs and engravings of old European kitchen gardens. Recent restoration programs have returned many of these magnificent gardens to their former glory, allowing us to glean inspiration from the old master gardeners. The traditional walled Victorian kitchen garden at Chilton Foliat in Berkshire, England, and the grand potager at Chateau de Villandry, France, were two of the beautifully restored

kitchen gardens that started us thinking about our own vegetable garden in a new way.

We didn't have the time, space, or desire to care for a large, sprawling garden. However, on a much smaller scale, we were inspired to transform our simple plot of vegetables into a visually stunning kitchen garden that reflected the old-world elegance of the European kitchen gardens. As we began designing our garden—mingling flowers, herbs, and vegetables—we followed the same important rules European gardeners adhered to centuries before: attention to detail, artistic presentation, and color coordination. The result is a beautiful, productive kitchen garden that we proudly display in the center of our landscape.

It's important to note that you don't have to seek your inspiration for design ideas from gardens of the past. If you open up your imagination, potential designs for kitchen gardens are ubiquitous. An heirloom quilt, a Japanese family crest, or a piece of honeycomb can all be the catalyst for what just may be your best garden ever.

The kitchen gardens presented in this book walk a fine line between ornamental gardens and productive vegetable gardens. The majority of the flowers used are not edible, and many of the vegetables are used for their ornamental beauty. There's no arguing that your garden would produce two to three times more vegetables if you laid it out in conventional, straight rows, but we look at the value of our harvest in both aesthetic and utilitarian terms.

This book is a culmination of our experimentation. It's a guide for designing practical, productive, and aesthetically pleasing kitchen gardens. The book takes you step-by-step from inspiration and design through installation and harvest. Whether you design your own kitchen garden or use the patterns we present here, you can create a beautiful and productive kitchen garden.

Nine large squares comprise Chateau de Villandry's kitchen garden, with each square having a different design.

PHOTO COURTESY OF CHATEAU DE VILLANDRY, TOURS, FRANCE.

chapter one

Lessons from the Past

*g*ardens have been an inextricable part of nearly every culture since the dawn of antiquity. All of our contemporary garden styles, whether aesthetic or utilitarian in nature, have evolved throughout the centuries by building on the designs and creativity of those who came before us. Every culture adds its own distinctive mark to this evolution, being influenced by new inventions, discoveries, and social attitudes. Most of us, however, are unaware of any part we might be playing in this continually unfolding story. Yet each spring, the much-anticipated and simple process of choosing plants and designing how our gardens will look links us to a rich, unbroken chain of horticultural history.

GARDEN DESIGNS THROUGHOUT HISTORY

Kitchen gardens have experienced their own distinctive evolution throughout the centuries. Without question, they have mainly served a very practical purpose for most people: to provide a bountiful harvest of fresh vegetables. But, with human nature being as it is, there has often been the desire to lift the basic vegetable garden to a level of beauty more characteristic of ornamental flower gardens. The inspiration necessary for creating our own unique kitchen gardens can be found throughout history: from the French kitchen gardens, or *potagers*, of the 16th and 17th centuries, to the informal cottage gardens of England.

But the scope of influence on our garden designs need not be limited only to the kitchen gardens of the past. Instead, we can easily adapt, at least in part, any of the great ornamental garden designs for use in our landscapes. Naturally, the expansive tree-lined walkways, or *allées,* of Versailles would not translate into a backyard setting, but a simplified pattern based on one of the many beautiful parterres might.

Today we have the wonderful opportunity to study a wide variety of gardens from throughout history and adapt them for use in our own kitchen gardens.

Roman gardens

Many of the great European garden designs have their roots in the patrician gardens of ancient Rome. Romans were originally farmers and traders with an identity linked firmly to the land. But as their empire grew, so did the aristocracy. To escape the increasingly crowded city, many of Rome's wealthier residents established villas by the sea or near the foothills of the Apennines. Their penchant for pleasure produced what may have been the first gardens grown exclusively for aesthetics instead of for food, medicine, or symbolic reasons.

Pliny the Younger (62-113) was a wealthy Roman statesman who built several villas in the countryside near Rome. Through his letters we get an idea of the size and complexity of the gardens he established. They included expansive, geometrically shaped garden beds, ponds, fountains, borders of box and laurel, and animal-shaped topiaries.

Pliny's letters give us a view of what was characteristic of many Roman villas of the time. Gardens became a source of pleasure and relaxation. They were treated as extensions of the home and were valued primarily for their beauty and ornamentation. This break from a more-utilitarian past laid the groundwork for many of the great gardens that followed.

Our kitchen gardens are unique and manageable in size, yet they possess design elements that link them to garden designs of the past.

Medieval monastic gardens

With the fall of the Roman Empire (approximately 500), Europe entered the Middle Ages, a period of relative stagnation and strict feudalism. The Middle Ages would last for approximately 1,000 years until the humanistic flame was rekindled at the beginning of the Renaissance.

Monasteries were established throughout Europe during the Middle Ages and were crucial in preserving the sum of man's knowledge since ancient times. By carefully copying and maintaining old manuscripts, the monastic monks kept alive information that may have otherwise been lost, including Roman horticultural practices.

The monks were self-sufficient, growing all their own medicinal herbs, fruits, vegetables, and flowers.

This is the garden plan of Pliny the Younger's villa in Tuscany, drawn in the 18th century by Robert Castell.

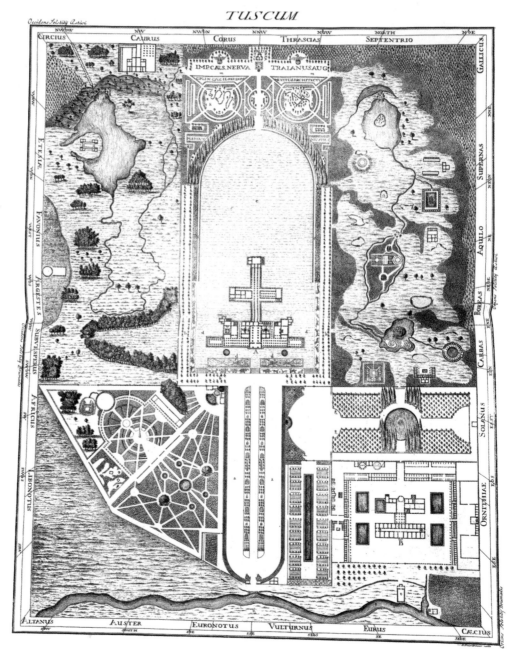

Although segregated into separate parts, the herbs, fruits, vegetables, and flowers were generally grown together within one cloister, or enclosed, garden.

The garden was typically a simple geometrical design, usually containing four sections: a physic garden for medicinal herbs; a combined orchard and vineyard; a vegetable garden consisting of square or rectangular beds (edged with boards or willow branches) that enabled the monks to maintain the beds from a network of paths, thus avoiding soil compaction; and a flower garden containing plants such as violets, Madonna lilies, and roses, which were grown for their fragrance and religious symbolism and were used to decorate the altar.

Like monastic gardens of the Middle Ages, the vegetables at Chateau de Villandry are planted in blocks rather than in rows.
COREL STOCK PHOTO.

Italian Renaissance gardens

During the pre-Renaissance period in the 14th century, Europe was gradually awakening to a new age of humanistic thought. New trade and exploration, a resurgent interest in the arts and sciences preserved from ancient Greece and Rome, and greater freedom to explore new ideas and new ways of thinking were firmly taking root. Approaches to horticulture were also breaking free from the confinement of medieval cloister gardens.

Simple herb and boxwood parterres, garden rooms, and water features were just a few of the classical elements of Italian Renaissance gardens.

COREL STOCK PHOTO.

By the 16th century, Italian garden architects were creating beautiful new villas inspired by the Roman gardens of Pliny the Younger and others. Many of these grand estates were situated on steep hillsides, which took advantage of sweeping views and cool breezes. The steep terrain on which the villas were built also inspired elaborate, gravity-powered water features such as fountains, jets, basins, and waterfalls.

In keeping with the rebirth of a more-humanistic philosophy, gardens were constructed once again for pleasure instead of for purely utilitarian purposes. Garden designers incorporated outdoor living spaces, or "rooms," as extensions of the villas. Multilevel terraces helped delineate separate areas, such as outdoor theaters, exercise cloisters, and dining terraces. A secluded garden, or *giardino segreto,* was usually adjacent to the villa and included flowers, herbs, and sometimes whimsical topiaries. This enclosed garden offered the owner of the villa a private retreat. While the main gardens typically contained decorative flowers, herbs, boxwood, and fruit and nut trees, vegetables were relegated to separate, more-utilitarian garden plots.

Also reminiscent of the villas of ancient Rome was the inclusion of symmetry and simple geometric shapes into the garden landscape. Terraces were adorned with potted plants, parterres of clipped herbs and boxwood hedges, Roman-style statues, and well-manicured topiaries.

With the age of exploration well underway, many new plant varieties were being discovered and collected from distant lands and brought back

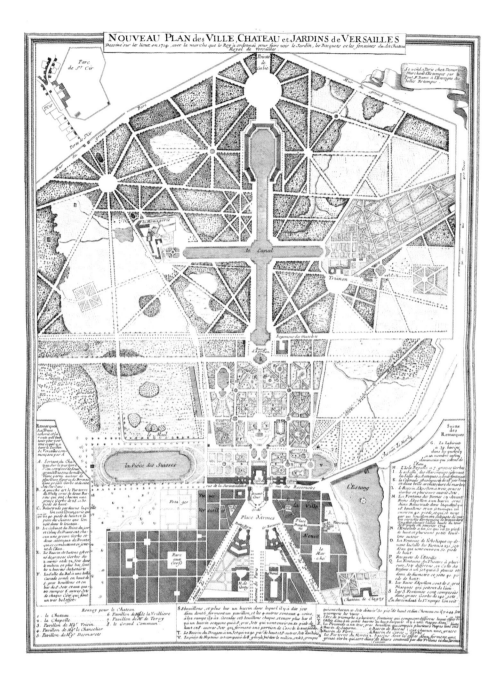

NOUVEAU PLAN des VILLE, CHATEAU et JARDINS de VERSAILLES

Pierre Le Pautre's 1717 plan of Versailles illustrates the impressive size and details of the gardens.

to Italy. The first botanical gardens were developed to make available these new species of plants for scientific study. And wealthy estate owners were quick to incorporate the colorful, new, and exotic flowers and bulbs into their geometrically designed boxwood parterres.

The reemergence of grand garden design in Italy during the early Renaissance was not destined to remain only within the Italian border. The influence of these new Italian gardens spread quickly to England, Germany, Holland, Spain, and France, with each country adapting these designs to its own unique environment and topography.

French formal gardens

Perhaps nothing exemplifies the grand formal gardens of France during the "Age of Kings" more than Versailles, built in the second half of the 17th century. But the seed for this magnificent garden was sown more than 150 years earlier during the reign of Charles VIII (1483-1498), who brought in Italian artisans and craftsmen to work on the castle at Amboise. During the 16th century, the Italian Renaissance continued to influence the design of many grand chateaus, including Louis XII's castle at Blois and Francis I's castle at Fontainebleau.

Many gardens during this period were a hybrid of styles bearing the lingering influence of medieval cloister gardens, the geometrically shaped parterres of Italian Renaissance gardens, and the many unique influences dictated by French culture and the country's terrain.

The Chateau de Villandry is a good example of a 16th-century chateau. It was reconstructed during the first part of this century by Dr. Joachim Carvallo based on the engravings of Jacques Androuet du Cerceau (1520-1585). Today, the nine squares of the spectacular kitchen garden comprise the lowest of three terraces. Similar to the monastic gardens of the Middle Ages, the vegetables are grown in blocks rather than in rows. Flower beds frame the large squares while rose bowers and central fountains further suggest the medieval influence. The middle terrace contains the "love garden," comprised of four large squares of flower-filled boxwood designs depicting four types of love: *l'amour tendre* (tender), *l'amour tragique* (tragic), *l'amour volage* (fickle), and *l'amour folie* (mad). Vineyards, orchards, and a reflecting pond are located on the uppermost terrace.

By the 17th century, French garden architects were creating gardens that were uniquely French and breathtaking in scope. Claud Mollet, gardener to Henry IV and later to Louis XIII, took the Italian Renaissance concept of a simple geometric parterre and created the *parterre de broderie*, reminiscent of fine embroidery. Mollet used precisely clipped boxwood hedges to create intricate scrollwork patterns. Grass and crushed stone, sand, or earth of various colors filled the spaces between the boxwood hedges. Flowers were used in thin bands around the perimeter, framing the parterre.

André Le Nôtre, commissioned by the Sun King, Louis XIV, to help design and build the gardens of Versailles, used the same style of parterres in this expansive 250-acre project. It took more than 40 years to complete and required the labor of several thousand men. Symmetry, linear perspective, and ornamentation were the hallmarks of French formality. Le Nôtre used all of these components to design and locate sweeping terraces, canals, tree-lined allées, ornate fountains, statues, and symmetrical parterres.

Le Nôtre used the tall, architectural structure of clipped evergreens, as well as trees potted in tubs, as vertical counterpoints to the low-lying parterres. Because of the popularity of parterres, books were published containing parterre patterns to be used by aspiring gardeners. In Alexandre Le Blond's 1728 book *Theory and Practice of Gardening,* he suggested design ideas for parterres, including knots, clasps, cartouches, and flower and foliage motifs.

During the 17th century, kitchen gardens were still segregated from the ornamental gardens of the chateaus and palaces. This was the case at Versailles. However, the king's kitchen garden was no less impressive. The area allocated for the royal fruit and vegetable garden was originally a swampy plot of land. It first had to be drained and filled with cartloads of soil and manure to improve the acreage before construction of the garden could begin.

Jean de la Quintinie designed and helped build the 20-acre kitchen garden at Versailles between 1677 and 1683. The center was sunken and geometrically arranged into 16 raised beds. The perimeter was sectioned off into 29 separate walled gardens to create a warmer, more-protected environment for growing fruit trees. Like all the other orna-mental trees at Versailles, they too were meticulously pruned and shaped into fancy espaliers.

To protect vulnerable potted citrus trees during the cold winter months, an orangery was also built at Versailles. Orangeries generally had large windows on three sides and were heated with wood or coal. Unlike greenhouses and conservatories, orangeries had traditional roofs. Through the use of the orangery, walled gardens, and cold frames, la Quintinie provided the king with year-round crops.

The style of French formality quickly spread throughout Europe. The Palace of Het Loo in the Netherlands is a good example. Constructed between 1685 and 1700, William of Orange and Mary Stewart used Het Loo as a hunting seat. William hired 24-year-old Daniel Marot, a French Huguenot and gifted designer and engraver, to design the magnificent parterres de broderie.

English gardens

At the beginning of the 16th century, knot gardens became popular in England. Closely paralleling similarly designed gardens in Italy at the time, these intricately woven knot gardens were formed from ribbons of rosemary, thyme, and hyssop (dwarf boxwood was used later in the 17th century).

If the knot design was filled in with flowers, having no pathways within the garden, it was called a closed knot. If pathways of grass, stones, sand, or brick were incorporated as part of the design, it was called an open knot. Pattern books were also published for knot-garden designs, and these gardens remained popular for over 100 years.

By the early 17th century, French formal designs were strongly influencing gardens in England. The garden at Wilton, designed by Isaac de Caus in 1615, had many French influences, including its parterre de broderie. And perhaps the best evidence of the continental influence were the gardens at Hampton Court during the reign of William and Mary. Here, the sway of the Mollet family was clearly evident in the goose-foot pattern, or *patte d'oie*, of tree-lined allées and the large parterre de broderie. But a new century was at hand, and the geometric grandeur that belonged to the 17th century was soon to be deposed.

Early in the 18th century, during the reign of Queen Anne (1702-1714), the formal gardens of the past century were swept away by an overwhelming call for more natural-looking landscapes. Many writers made fun of popular topiaries. Joseph Addison, for instance, labeled them "vegetable sculptures." And

A background of colored stones illuminates the parterre de broderie, while the flower beds and cone-shaped yews and junipers frame the pattern and add height.

PHOTO BY R. MULDER, COURTESY OF PALEIS HET LOO, NATIONAL MUSEUM, APELDOORN, THE NETHERLANDS.

the poet Alexander Pope mused, "A quickset hog, shot up into a porcupine, by being forgot a week in rainy weather."

Many of the formal gardens of England were being refashioned by emerging landscape designers such as William Kent and Lancelot "Capability" Brown. The tight control and geometric vistas of Le Nôtre were replaced by soft contours and gentle curves. Straight allées were replaced by more-natural clusters of trees although still very purposefully planted to frame the landscape. This open and parklike style was to influence many of the great public parks and estates in America, including Central Park in New York City. Trade with the Orient also had a major impact on garden design during this period, as traders and missionaries brought back news of naturalistic gardens in Japan and China.

In the 19th century, during the long reign of Queen Victoria (1837-1901), new discoveries inspired innovative designs for English gardens. Professional plant hunters traveled the world, collecting hundreds of new specimens of trees, shrubs, and annuals. Seedsmen and nurseries sprang up all over England to propagate, hybridize, and distribute these new specimens.

Annuals, both newly discovered and those introduced in the 18th century, offered gardeners an array of colors. Vibrant flowers, including salvia, lobelia, zinnias,

At the Smithsonian Institution in Washington, D.C., low-growing annuals create a colorful carpet effect similar to the designs of the Victorian era.

gazanias, pelargoniums, calceolarias, petunias, and verbenas, added to the excitement. Large blocks of these annuals were used to form flamboyant designs, such as concentric circles or ribbon borders resembling colorful carpets (hence the name "carpet bedding").

In the mid-1800s, sheet-glass manufacturing was invented, and greenhouses became very popular. The greenhouses enabled seedsmen, nurseries, and gardeners to raise tender annual species from around the world. As the glass became less expensive, greenhouses became more accessible to the middle class, allowing them to join in the frenzy of raising bedding plants.

By the late 19th century, there was a movement once again toward an informal, natural style of gardening,

with advocates such as William Robinson and Gertrude Jekyll. The advocates of this movement viewed the carpet-bedding techniques of the mid-Victorian era as garish and far too busy, preferring a garden more closely tied to the classic English cottage garden.

The cottage garden used hardy perennials in mixed borders to produce lasting color throughout the growing season. Unlike carpet bedding, perennial borders contained plants of varying heights, textures, and forms, and great attention was paid to harmonious color schemes. This style of gardening is still a major influence in many gardens throughout the world today.

Today, carpet-bedding designs are often seen in parks depicting flags, words, or, in this case, a floral clock.

COREL STOCK PHOTO.

Historical Influences in Our Kitchen Garden

At first, it may seem that Pliny the Younger's villa in Tuscany or Le Nôtre's plan for Versailles could have little or no relevance to a 20-ft. by 20-ft. square of garden soil lying just beyond the kitchen window. But these ancient plans and styles can be used to provide us with a wealth of inspiration and usable designs.

For instance, we were able to incorporate many design aspects from historical gardens into our own kitchen gardens. The photos on these pages show some characteristics that our gardens share with those of the past.

Similar to the monastic gardens of the Middle Ages, our garden beds are small and easily maintained from the paths. Here, endive is being blanched under pots.

Italian Renaissance gardeners used boxwood hedges to create simple geometric designs. We used fast-growing parsley in our kitchen gardens as a boxwood substitute.

To add a formal ambience to our gardens similar to the formal gardens of 17th-century France, we carefully laid out the geometrical designs.

English gardeners of the Victorian era massed annual bedding plants to create designs. We used annuals to delineate our patterns.

Like the colored stones and sand in the parterres de broderie of France, paths of sawdust, gravel, and bark chips add color to our designs.

Use your imagination to create vivid kitchen-garden designs.

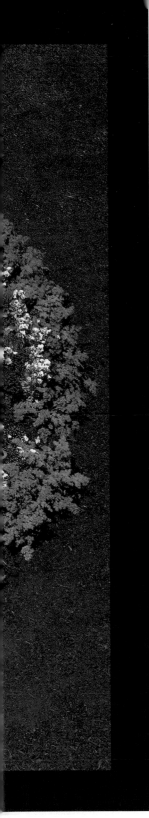

Designing Your Kitchen Garden

*d*esigning a new kitchen garden is always exciting. The process begins as a simple idea that quickly germinates when the first seed catalogs arrive in midwinter. As you pore over the pages, rich photos of colorful blooms and sumptuous vegetables inspire your imagination. The enticing copy extols: "Sweet buttery taste!" "Crisp texture and intense flavor!" "Literally covered with magnificent blossoms all summer!" You may want to buy every variety of seed in each catalog, but your ideal kitchen garden will result only from a well-thought-out plan.

Each spring provides us with the opportunity to start new gardens, expand existing ones, and test our imaginations. This chapter will give you specific ideas, plans, instructions, and inspiration for designing your own distinctive kitchen garden.

A DESIGN FOR EVERY KITCHEN GARDEN

The available area for your new kitchen garden may be as small as a window box, or it may encompass your entire backyard. Irrespective of size, there is an exquisite design for every garden. The following pages have photographs and plans for small, medium-size, and large kitchen gardens. Each photograph is accompanied by a measured grid of the garden plan (most of which show the placement of stakes and string to outline the beds) and an illustration indicating the placement of specific plants. Together with an accompanying plant list, you can easily re-create any one of these gardens or use them as inspiration to design your own.

The bold, gray-green foliage of a large cardoon is the main attraction in this container arrangement.

Ideas for a small kitchen garden

Great things come in small packages, and a small kitchen garden is no exception. A well-designed window box or half whiskey barrel, overflowing with lush vegetables and cascading flowers, can be a dazzling addition to a landscape or an apartment terrace. Similarly, small raised beds can provide a visual feast and a surprising amount of produce at harvest time.

Our definition of a small garden is a growing area 36 sq. ft. or less. A garden of this size will limit the types of plants you can grow and the types of garden features (if any) you can have. However, the advantages a small garden has over a large one will more than compensate for these restrictions.

Low maintenance is a small garden's strength. Every part of the garden is within arm's reach, allowing for easy cultivation, planting, weeding, watering, and harvesting. Weeding is perhaps the most time-consuming garden task. But in a small garden, this chore is all but eliminated because the closely grouped plants shade out the weeds. And with a lack of weeds, these compact and tidy growing areas rarely draw large pest populations. A small garden is perfect for busy people with limited time for garden maintenance.

Another big advantage of a small kitchen garden is its moderate cost. Paths are not necessary in a small garden, eliminating the need for paving materials. And, with only a few inexpensive seed packets or trays of vegetable and flower seedlings, you can grow an abundance of leafy greens and fragrant flowers throughout the summer.

A window box is a charming addition to a home and can provide growing space for vegetables.

Cost considerations are important, but carefully planning a small garden is essential. To create a captivating display, flower textures and colors must be determined while also leaving room for vegetable production. Herein lies a fun design puzzle.

To get the most from a small garden, keep to low-growing, compact varieties that conserve space, such as lettuce, parsley, pansies, and lobelia. Successive plantings of short-season crops like radishes and spinach will also increase your harvest. Planting the seedlings a bit closer together than you normally would not only

conserves space but also gives a small garden a lush, abundant look. Trellising vines and tall vegetables, like cucumbers and tomatoes, will let you take advantage of vertical space, allowing you to grow more varieties on less soil. With these parameters in mind, you can see why a small garden makes a wonderful salad garden.

Along with color, texture, and space, proportion plays an integral part in the design of a small kitchen garden. For example, a 2-ft. window box and a 16-in. clay pot have approximately the same cubic capacity; however, their proportions are vastly

different. A towering cardoon or artichoke plant would look entirely out
of place in a window box, but either
one would look quite elegant in a
large clay pot. As a general rule of
thumb, the height of the tallest plant
should be no more than two times
the height of the container. The
chart on p. 91 that show the colors,
textures, and heights of various
plants and vegetables, will be especially helpful when selecting plants
for containers and small gardens.

Window box

A window box filled with flowers and
vegetables is a beautiful addition to
the exterior of any house and provides a charming view from inside
(see the grid, drawing, and plant list
on the facing page). In addition, you
can harvest an abundance of fresh
produce from your window box if a
few important growing requirements
are met.

A sunny location is the most important requirement. For instance, a
window under an eave or awning
may be inappropriate for a window
box because of the shadows these
structures cast. For maximum sun exposure, position your box beneath a
south-, west-, or east-facing window.
Your climate will determine the best
location. For example, in warm cli-
mates, a south-facing window may be
too hot for growing lettuce.

Drill several drainage holes in the
box (our own box has four $\frac{1}{2}$-in.
drainage holes covered with screen
to retain the soil) and fill it with
loose, well-draining potting soil.
Once you have the window box planted, check on it often. The combination of a sunny exposure and the
box's limited soil capacity will dry out
the soil quickly, and daily watering
may be necessary. But daily watering
will leach nutrients from the soil, so
you'll have to add an organic fertilizer to the soil throughout the growing
season (follow the instructions on the
fertilizer label).

Small, compact herb and vegetable
varieties such as lettuce, chives, and
basil work well within the confines of
a window box. Shallow root crops
like green onions, radishes, and baby
carrots can also be grown successfully. The flowers should be small and
compact or of a trailing nature. Plant
them close to the edges and let them
spill over the sides as they grow,
which conserves space while softening the hard lines of the window box.

We located our window boxes
beneath west-facing windows. The
pansies, petunias, and lobelia
mingled among the lettuce, green
onions, and parsley, which created
an appealing and appetizing display
and lent a cottage feeling to the front
of our studio.

Window-Box Garden

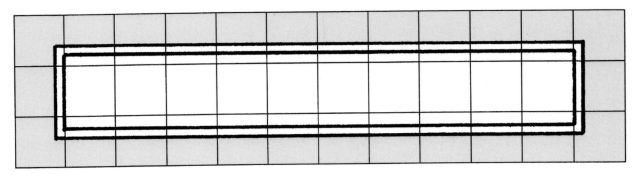

I square = 6 in.
Shaded areas are not planted.

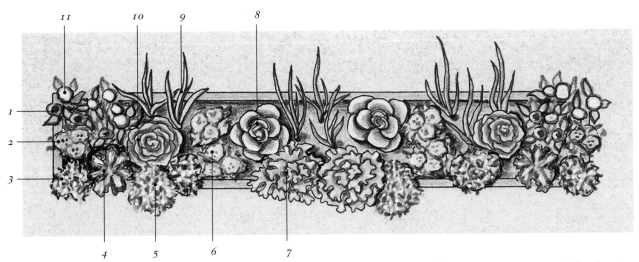

*Illustration represents general plant location.
For actual numbers, refer to the plant list.*

PLANT LIST

Plant	How many
1. Purple petunia	2
2. Pink pansy	3
3. Magenta lobelia	4
4. Parsley	2
5. Blue lobelia	2
6. Yellow pansy	3
7. Green oak-leaf lettuce	2
8. Cos lettuce	2
9. Onion	9
10. Red-leaf lettuce	2
11. White petunia	4

Half whiskey barrel

A half whiskey barrel offers economical growing options to the gardener with limited space. You can use the barrel on its own, or you can attach a trellis to it for growing vines or tall vegetables. By planting a small plot of ground around the base of the barrel, you can create a multilevel garden. We used all three growing areas, and the result was an impressive array of flowers and vegetables in a small 4-ft. by 5-ft. garden (see the photo on the facing page).

When making a half-whiskey-barrel garden, your first job will be to drill six, ½-in. holes in the bottom of the barrel and then cover the holes with a piece of screen. The screen will retain soil while allowing for drainage. Then fill the barrel with loose, well-draining soil, and you are ready for planting. A half whiskey barrel is very similar to a window box in its plant selection, placement, and maintenance requirements: Compact varieties are best, keep the flowers to the edges, water often, and fertilize.

We grew root crops around the base of our barrel and several calendula plants (see the grid, drawing, and plant list on p. 28). Cherry tomatoes adorned the trellis, and beneath

Edible flower petals, such as calendula and nasturtium, will brighten up any green salad.

it we grew lettuce, green onions, parsley, alyssum, and nasturtium. We trained the nasturtium to grow up the tomato trellis. Interlaced with one another, the red and orange flowers were a perfect color match to the ripening cherry tomatoes. This small garden was visually striking and supplied us with fresh salads and edible flower garnishes all summer long.

In this half-whiskey-barrel garden, six varieties of vegetables (lettuce, cherry tomatoes, onions, parsley, carrots, and radishes) are growing among the profusion of flowers.

Half-Whiskey-Barrel Garden

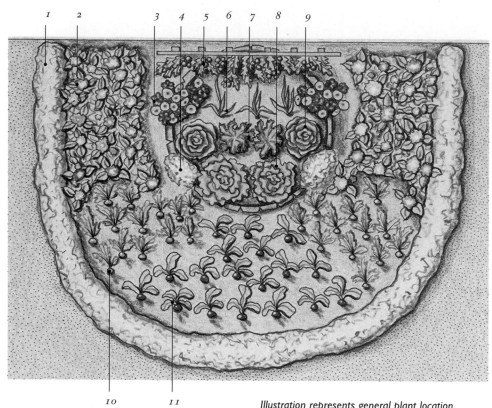

Illustration represents general plant location.
For actual numbers, refer to the plant list.

PLANT LIST

Plant	How many
1. White alyssum	24
2. Calendula (tall and dwarf)	12
3. Nasturtium	4
4. White alyssum	2
5. Cherry tomato	1
6. Yellow onion	4
7. Parsley	2
8. Green oak-leaf lettuce	2
9. Red-leaf lettuce	2
10. Carrot	24
11. Radish	15

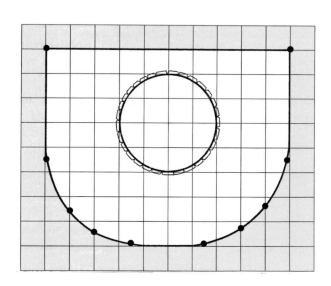

1 square = 6 in.
Shaded areas are not planted.
Dots indicate stake placement for bed layout.

Small-scale designs work perfectly in a raised bed. Here, large red and green cabbage plants create a central focal point.

Raised beds

For versatility, low maintenance, and aesthetic appeal, raised beds provide a marvelous option for small-scale kitchen gardening. A raised bed is a cross between container gardening and planting in the open ground and possesses the best traits of both.

Similar to a container garden, the soil in a raised bed drains freely and warms quickly for early spring planting. Comparable to a garden in the open ground, all varieties of root crops can be successfully grown in a raised bed.

Measuring only 5 ft. by 7 ft. (see the grid below), our small raised bed, with its delicate flower borders, looked wonderful all summer and produced an impressive harvest. We combined the flowers and vegetables to create a simple yet elegant pattern. Lavender ageratum, dusty miller, and yellow pansies subtly complimented the violet and gray-green shades of the red and green cabbage.

The corner triangles contained a succession of short-season crops (see the drawing and plant list on the fac-ing page). We started in early spring with spinach and green onions and later replaced them with radishes and lettuce. Although the cabbage plants monopolized a large portion of the raised bed, their large ruffled leaves and elegant colors created a beautiful centerpiece to the design.

Ideas for a medium-size kitchen garden

The size and manageability of a medium-size kitchen garden make it perfect for a family. We define a medium-size garden as a growing area measuring from 36 sq. ft. up to 625 sq. ft. A garden of this size is large enough to grow a variety of veg-etables, yet it is not overwhelming. A few hours a week weeding, watering, and harvesting will keep the garden meticulously maintained.

Diversity is a medium-size garden's forte. It can be planted solely with annuals, or it can accommodate a few well-placed perennials. Unlike a small garden, a medium-size garden has space for structures and garden features. Trellises can be used around the garden's perimeter for training vines or for supporting tall crops such as beans, peas, and tomatoes. There's even enough room for a sundial or a judiciously placed statue. The center of the garden, however, will look best if it is planted with low-growing flowers and vegeta-bles such as alyssum, lobelia, lettuce, and cabbage.

A medium-size garden will need paths (or stepping pads) so you can gain access to the garden's interior. But the paths only need to be wide enough for one person to walk through. These narrow paths define the garden while conserving precious growing space.

Grid for Raised-Bed Garden

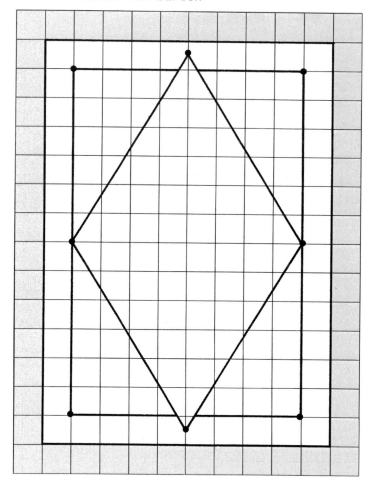

I square = 6 in.
Shaded areas are not planted.
Dots indicate stake placement for bed layout.

Raised-Bed Garden

*Illustration represents general plant location.
For actual numbers, refer to the plant list.*

PLANT LIST

Plant	How many
1. Dusty miller	48
2. Lavender ageratum	38
3. Cos lettuce	2
4. Radish	24
5. Green cabbage	2
6. Red cabbage	2
7. Yellow pansy	32
8. Yellow onion	10
9. Red-leaf lettuce	3

For a larger harvest, keep a succession of crops growing. In early spring, when the cabbage plants are small, plant up to six heads of lettuce in the center bed. Harvest them as the cabbage plants mature and need more room. Keep the corner triangles rotating with short-season salad crops such as spinach, green onions, radishes, and lettuce.

In this white-diamond design, paths crisscross through snowy borders of alyssum and beds of vegetables.

White-diamond and purple-star gardens

We blended ornamental design with vegetable production to create two 16-ft. by 18-ft. gardens that were totally annual in nature (see the photos above and on the facing page). We mulched the paths with biodegradable wood shavings, which allowed the gardens to be completely turned under at the end of the season. The compact beds were easy to maintain

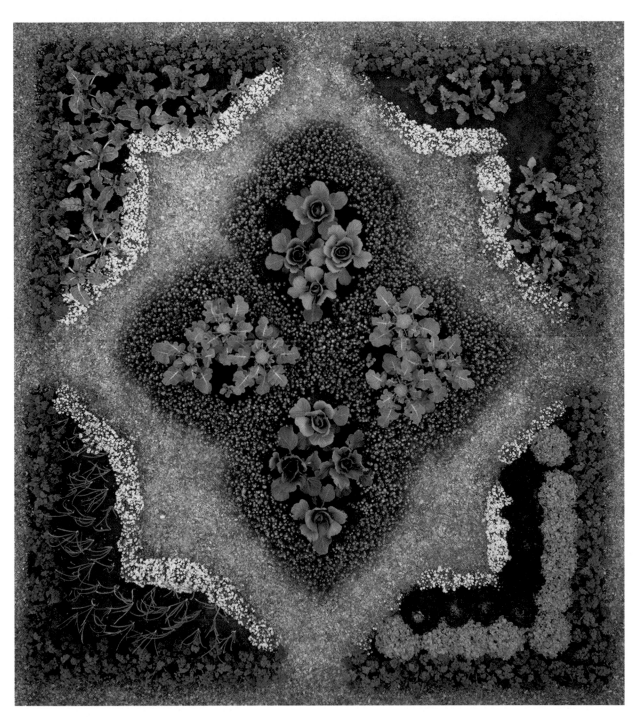

*This brilliant
purple-star design
is framed by
perimeter beds
of leafy greens.*

yet produced an abundance of fresh
vegetables throughout the summer
and fall.

   We selected low-growing, compact
plants and placed them close together. Low-growing plants hold the de-

sign unlike tall plants, which tend to
break up the design. We placed large-
leaf broccoli and cabbage plants in
the middle of each garden as bold
centerpieces. Framing the center
beds of each garden were perimeter

Large, gray-green cabbage and broccoli plants are surrounded by a profusion of purple alyssum.

cluttered. Both gardens were bordered with a "formal hedge" of vivid green parsley.

We wanted to keep the growing areas to a maximum and the path widths to a minimum, so we made the paths 18 in. to 24 in. wide. They were comfortable to walk on as long as we kept the borders neatly trimmed back with grass clippers. By fall, all of the vegetables were harvested, yet the designs remained until the first hard frost, carried on by the paths and borders (see the grids, drawings, and plant lists on pp. 36 and 37).

Ideas for a large kitchen garden

For the ambitious kitchen gardener with plenty of space, a large garden offers unlimited possibilities. Our definition of a large garden is a growing area approximately 625 sq. ft. or larger. Unlike a small or medium-size garden that is *placed within* the landscape, a large kitchen garden, in many cases, *becomes* the landscape. Therefore, a large garden must be designed with outdoor living in mind. This includes wider paths for easy access to beds, areas for structures and garden features that will be used for both practical and aesthetic purposes, and, perhaps, an area designated for outdoor furniture.

Although a large garden could be entirely annual in nature and turned under at year's end, it is more efficient to eliminate yearly replotting and install a permanent framework of paths and garden beds. A garden with a permanent framework has many advantages. It allows you to plant perennial vegetables, herbs, and berries and to keep a yearly crop-

beds planted with lettuce, beets, onions, and white Swiss chard.

We created the elegant look of both gardens by using only one or two colors and plant varieties in the borders. The white-diamond pattern used only white alyssum, while the purple-star design used purple and white alyssum and lobelia. Too many colors and plant types would have made these gardens look busy and

rotation schedule. The paths can be constructed from easily maintained, nonbiodegradable materials such as gravel or brick.

A large garden also offers a variety of planting options. The expanse of space lets you grow a broader range of plants, including sprawling vines such as cucumbers and squash, large plants like artichokes, and tall plants such as trellised tomatoes. The placement of plants can also be varied. Unlike a small or medium-size garden, large and tall plants can be placed strategically throughout a large kitchen garden rather than being restricted to perimeter beds. Just remember to evaluate the amount of shadow these plants will cast before placing them.

A large garden area can quickly get out of control, so punctual maintenance is particularly important. A weekly weeding routine will keep a large area neat and therefore relatively pest free. Harvesting also needs to be done on a regular basis. Have a well-thought-out plan for the vegetables you choose because a large garden produces a copious amount of produce, and you can quickly be overwhelmed. A successive planting schedule will help spread your harvest over the entire summer.

White-Diamond Garden

Illustration represents general plant location. For actual numbers, refer to the plant list.

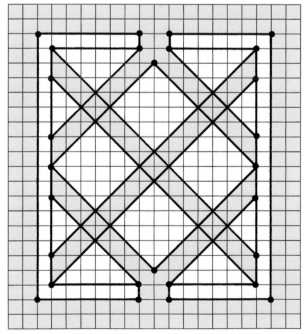

1 square = 1 ft.
Shaded areas are not planted.
Dots indicate stake placement for bed layout.

Purple-Star Garden

*Illustration represents
general plant location.
For actual numbers,
refer to the plant list.*

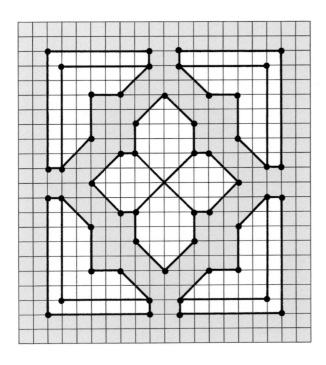

PLANT LIST

Plant	How many
1. Parsley	108
2. White Swiss chard	20
3. White alyssum	100
4. Purple alyssum	134
5. Blue lobelia	64
6. Broccoli	8
7. Yellow onion	30
8. Red cabbage	8
9. Green oak-leaf lettuce	10
10. Red-leaf lettuce	8
11. Beet	20

1 square = 1 ft.
Shaded areas are not planted.
Dots indicate stake placement for bed layout.

Feature garden

An engaging garden invites you to linger. We spent many weekend mornings enjoying coffee at a tiny table in our large kitchen garden. Breathing the fresh morning air while surrounded by a profusion of flowers, fruits, and vegetables was a delightful way to start the day.

Two 32-ft. by 32-ft. squares made up our large 32-ft. by 72-ft. kitchen garden. This amount of space let us incorporate a wide variety of plants and design elements into our garden plan. We chose plants ranging from annual staples like lettuce, broccoli, and carrots to perennial varieties such as blueberries, raspberries, and grapes. We also included an assortment of herbs to round out the garden's culinary palette (see the grids and plant lists on pp. 42 and 43).

We took advantage of the large space by adding a 3-ft.-wide border of cutting flowers along the garden's leading edge. Bright flower bouquets on the dinner table nicely complement our freshly picked vegetables.

Splitting the 32-ft. by 72-ft. growing area into two smaller gardens presented additional growing options. Connected by an 8-ft. grape and hop arbor, the two smaller gardens became separate garden "rooms." We planted them with two totally different color schemes and types of plants (see the drawings on pp. 40 and 41). The left side was planted with annuals in warm yellow, orange, and golden hues, while the right side consisted of cool violet and purple shades and was interplanted with perennials (see the photos on pp. 44 and 45). The juxtaposition of these complementary colors intensified the hues for a vivid contrasting effect. Even the paths reflected this contrast; we used the warm golden hues of sawdust on one side and cool gray shades of gravel on the other.

This large garden contained an arbor, several trellises, and six large clay pots. The paths were wide enough for the passage of a wheelbarrow and for a small table and a couple of chairs. The garden created a stunning outdoor living space while producing a culinary cornucopia.

Feature Garden

Warm Side

Cool Side

Grid for Warm Side of Feature Garden

I square = 2 ft.
Shaded areas are not planted.
Dots indicate stake placement
for bed layout.

PLANT LIST

WARM SIDE (p. 40)

Plant	How many	Plant	How many	Plant	How many
1. Pole bean	18	9. Yellow bush bean	23	21. Carrot	100
2. Winter squash	3	10. Butternut squash	3	22. White alyssum	296
3. Radicchio	24	11. Hop vines	2	23. Dwarf calendula	36
4. Yellow marigold	192	12. Butterhead lettuce	21	24. Zucchini (in large pots)	2
5. Dwarf sunflower	12	13. Zucchini	3	25. Ruby Swiss chard	32
6. Green bush bean	23	14. Endive	14	26. Golden beet	30
7. Yellow summer squash	3	15. Green oak-leaf lettuce	19	27. Tomato	4
8. Cutting border:		16. Orange marigold	160	28. Broccoli	9
Dusty miller	80	17. Red-leaf lettuce	12	29. Spinach	30
Sunflower	36	18. Yellow bell pepper	14	30. Cherry tomato	4
(tall and dwarf varieties)		19. Cucumber	8	31. Cos lettuce	4
Marigold	60	20. Green cabbage	9		
Bishop's flower	12				

Grid for Cool Side of Feature Garden

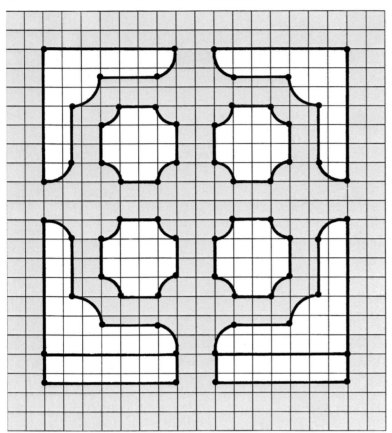

1 square = 2 ft.
Shaded areas are not planted.
Dots indicate stake placement
for bed layout.

PLANT LIST

COOL SIDE (p. 41)

Plant	How many	Plant	How many	Plant	How many
1. Morning glory	18	*10.* Herbs:		Pink pansy	3
2. Hen and chickens	54	Caraway	9	Purple alyssum	4
3. Blueberry bush	2	Green basil	16	*14.* Border flowers:	
4. Eggplant	8	Purple basil	7	Pink pansy	108
5. Raspberry cane	10	Chive	6	Magenta lobelia	108
6. Grapes and gourds:		Sage	2	Purple alyssum	216
Grape	2	Mint	1	*15.* Parsley	224
Gourd	4	Oregano	1	*16.* Red onion	48
7. Rhubarb	6	Dill	15	*17.* Red cabbage	9
8. Strawberry	6	Florence fennel	15	*18.* Magenta lobelia	180
9. Cutting border:		Cilantro	14	*19.* Kohlrabi	32
Dusty miller	80	Marjoram	6	*20.* Green cabbage	9
Aster	20	*11.* Ornamental kale	9	*21.* Violet cauliflower	9
Snapdragon	20	*12.* Blackberry vines	4	*22.* Leek	48
Zinnia	20	*13.* Container arrangements:		*23.* Broccoli	9
Scabiosa	20	Cardoon	1	*24.* Assorted potted plants	
Dianthus	20	Purple petunia	3		

In our feature garden, we grow a variety of herbs, including basil, parsley, sage, and dill, which can be used fresh or dried.

Pansies and lobelia are used in the feature garden to border young basil, oregano, and sage plants.

FINDING INSPIRATION FOR DESIGNS

Designing an ornamental kitchen garden begins with an idea for a pattern. You may already have a design idea in mind, or it may come to you as you doodle and sketch on graph paper. However, if you need some inspiration to get started, just look around. Garden designs are ubiquitous.

By looking around at everyday objects with an eye toward garden design, you will discover an amazing array of beautiful options. Your source of inspiration could be as literal as a past or present-day garden, or it could be hidden within the shapes in a quilt or a piece of architecture. We have listed a few good sources for design ideas, but if you use your imagination, you can find them anywhere.

Large outdoor arrangements are created with cut sunflowers, which are perfect for decorating a front porch or patio.

Asters, zinnias, snapdragons, and scabiosa provide a colorful flower border as well as many beautiful bouquets for indoors.

The trellises along the back fence of the feature garden support morning glories and pole beans.

The impressive kitchen garden at Chateau de Villandry has inspired many kitchen gardeners.

Grid for Villandry-Inspired Design

Past and present-day gardens

Studying great gardens, both past and present, can offer inspiration as well as an education (see Chapter 1). Years of planning, planting, growing, and experimenting have gone into the creation of these works of art. Much can be learned from examining their plant and color combinations, design elements, and the use of various landscape materials.

These expansive gardens are magnificent to admire and study, but few would be suitable for our busy lifestyles and small home landscapes. Fortunately, you can incorporate a few design elements you admire from these gardens into your smaller garden design, allowing you to create the same feeling but on a more manageable scale.

The magnificent kitchen garden at the Chateau de Villandry in France is an inspiration to consider (see the photo on the facing page). Nine individual squares comprise the entire garden, each with its own unique pattern. Intrigued by the idea, we designed four "minisquares" inspired by Villandry, each with its own pattern measuring 12 ft. square (see the grid above). If you have several design ideas in mind, this is a fun way to try them all in one year.

Plaid fabrics offer garden-design ideas complete with paths.

Fabrics

Inspiration for a garden design can also be found in any fabric store. Fabrics, buttons, and ribbons all present possibilities for patterns.

Components of your perfect garden design may be contained within a fabric's actual weave. If you look closely at plaid fabrics (see the photo at left), for instance, they offer wonderful proportions for parterres. The perpendicular lines are easily turned into a network of paths intersecting a series of square garden beds.

The garden design below left has four generously sized 8-ft. by 8-ft. beds. The plaid-inspired borders would look striking in two colors of low-growing flowers (indicated by dashed and solid lines). At the corners of the intersecting border lines, the flower colors can be woven together for an added plaid-fabric effect (see the Celtic knot garden on p. 63).

Grid for Plaid-Fabric-Inspired Design

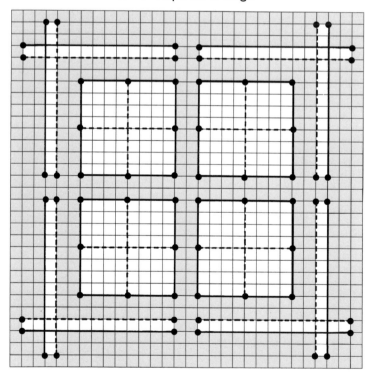

1 square = 1 ft.
Shaded areas are not planted.
Dots indicate stake placement for bed layout.
Low-growing flower borders are indicated by dashed and solid lines.

Quilts

The bold geometric shapes of a colorful fabric quilt translate beautifully into bold color blocks of flowers and vegetables in a garden design.

On graph paper, the individual shapes of a quilt block can be moved apart to allow for paths, or the pattern can be used as a garden design without any revisions. Paths are not necessary if you use several sections within the pattern as stepping pads.

We took the traditional pinwheel quilt pattern shown below and reworked the design to create a maze of paths (see the grid at right). We moved the triangles apart and scaled some down, yet the basic pinwheel pattern remained and was perfectly proportioned for garden beds.

Grid for Quilt-Inspired Design

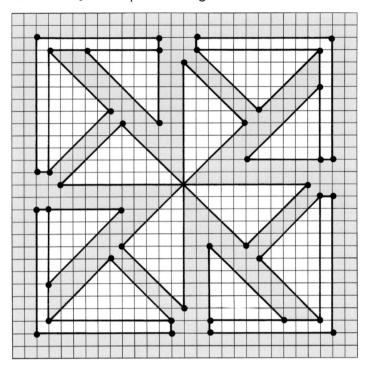

1 square = 1 ft.
*Shaded areas
are not planted.
Dots indicate
stake placement
for bed layout.*

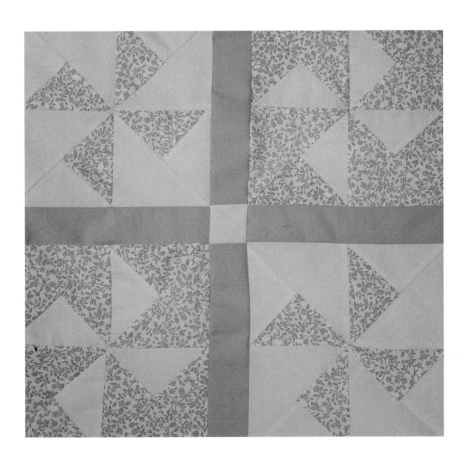

*Traditional quilt patterns
make wonderful geometrically
shaped gardens.*

Japanese designs

The beautiful artistry of the Japanese culture has long inspired designers. One source of that inspiration is the Japanese family crest. Dating back to the 11th century, these emblems were used on formal *kimonos* as symbols of family names. Both simple and elegant, they offer numerous possibilities as garden designs.

In a variety of kaleidoscopic shapes and interwoven patterns, many family crests could easily convert into parterres and knot gardens. We saw garden beds surrounded by a network of connecting paths in the family crest shown at right. The resulting design might be suitable for a small courtyard kitchen garden (see the grid below).

Japanese family crests, both simple and elegant, offer numerous possibilities as garden designs.

FROM *JAPANESE DESIGN MOTIFS*, DOVER PUBLICATIONS, INC.

Grid for Japanese Family-Crest-Inspired Design

I square = I ft.
Shaded areas are not planted.
Dots indicate stake placement for bed layout.

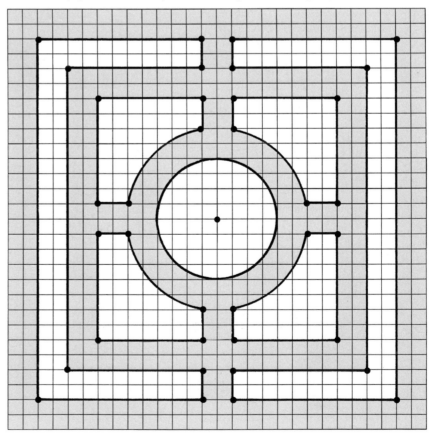

Celtic knot patterns

The intricate knotwork designs of the early Celtic artists were often created using mathematical formulas. Symbolizing eternity, the continuous line is the root of many of these designs. Throughout the centuries, Celtic art has embellished a variety of craft work such as stone monuments, jewelry, and metalwork. *The Book of Kells* is perhaps the most famous treasury of Celtic art.

You can create a stunning knot garden by simplifying a Celtic design. But to ensure your garden design stays manageable, use only a portion of a complex Celtic pattern. Keep in mind that the proportions may need expanding to allow enough room for garden beds and paths.

The Celtic design depicted on the embroidered broach shown below would look equally attractive as a garden design (see the grid at right). The artistic interlacing could be beautifully translated into colorful ribbons of alyssum or perhaps red- and green-leaf lettuce.

Grid for Celtic-Broach-Inspired Design

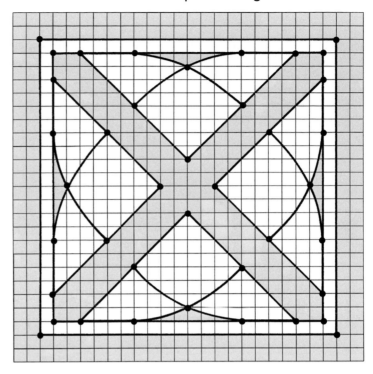

1 square = 1 ft.
Shaded areas are not planted.
Dots indicate stake placement for bed layout.

Traditional Celtic designs can inspire beautiful knot gardens.

Grid for Window-Inspired Design

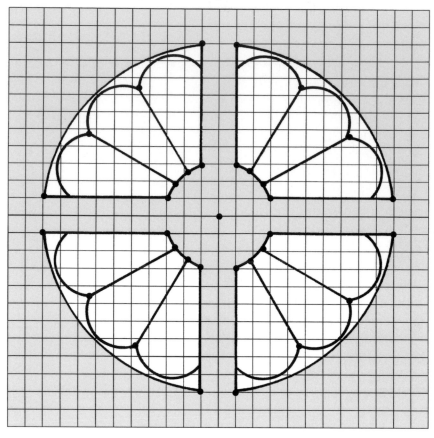

Architecture, from greenhouses to office buildings, can offer inspiration for garden designs.

1 square = 1 ft.
Shaded areas are not planted.
Dots indicate stake placement for bed layout.

Architecture

Many design elements contained in architecture are also present in good garden design. In both disciplines, proportion, scale, and rhythm are masterfully orchestrated to convey aesthetics.

Garden designers can easily find inspiration in the details of old architecture. For example, the shapes and proportions of a leaded-glass window may depict the configuration of several garden beds. Sculptured details on the exterior of an old office building might offer inspira-

tion for a labyrinth of paths. Old churches are especially rich in unique and interesting shapes, proportions, and patterns. From their beautiful stained-glass windows to the graceful arches of their cathedral ceilings, the design possibilities are almost limitless.

We thought it fitting to find several garden designs hidden in the architecture of the exquisite greenhouse shown above. For instance, by simply mirroring the front window's half-circle image, the resulting circular garden plan is a classic (see the grid above).

Everyday items

Use your imagination, and garden designs will appear all around you, from everyday objects to nature. The shape of an object, or a pattern on an object, might be your source of design inspiration. The fun is in the discovery!

Many city sidewalks have decorative iron grates that protect vulnerable tree roots. The iron is often cast into beautiful filigree patterns that may have knot-garden potential. Grates, jewelry, lace, china, tiles, and ironwork all possess possibilities.

Nature is also a limitless source of designs. Beautiful gardens can be designed from the shapes and patterns of snowflakes, leaves, and shells. We used the simple repeating hexagon pattern of honeycomb (see the photo at right) to create the center beds of the garden design below.

The simple repeating hexagon pattern of honeycomb can provide inspiration for garden designs.

Grid for Honeycomb-Inspired Design

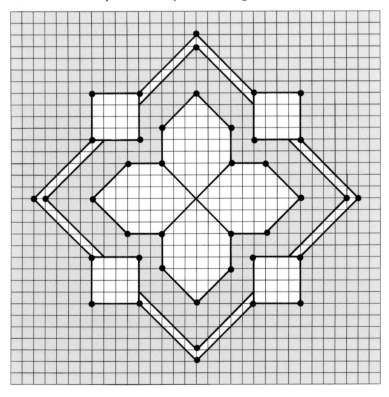

I square = 1 ft.
Shaded areas are not planted.
Dots indicate stake placement
for bed layout.

Flowers and vegetables combine to convey the feeling of a patchwork quilt.

Three inspirational garden designs

We took a quilt block, a Japanese family crest, and a Celtic knot pattern and turned them into kitchen gardens. The resulting garden trio is a tribute to these beautiful traditional designs and the cultures they represent. We planted each garden with a variety of annual flowers and vegetables and mulched the beds and paths with biodegradable peat moss and ground bark. At season's end, we completely turned under these gardens in preparation for new designs the following year.

Quilt block

The variable-star pattern is a traditional quilt-block design that easily converts to a garden (see the grid, drawing, and plant list on pp. 56 and 57). We used several triangles as stepping pads, making all areas of the garden accessible. The mulch on the stepping pads was an integral color component in the garden design. We chose rich, brown bark chips to complement the warm peach and yellow hues of the pansies and alyssum. The look evokes an image of an antique quilt—cozy enough to curl up under with a good garden book!

Quilt-Block Garden

*Illustration represents general plant location.
For actual numbers, refer to the plant list.*

Grid for Quilt-Block Garden

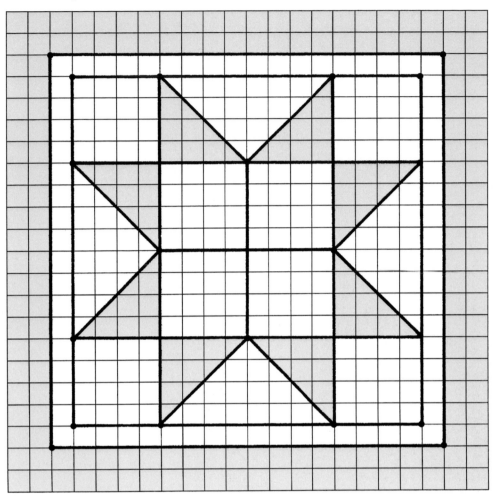

<table>
<tr><td colspan="4" align="center">PLANT LIST</td></tr>
<tr><td>Plant</td><td>How many</td><td>Plant</td><td>How many</td></tr>
<tr><td>1. Apricot pansy</td><td>248</td><td>8. Yellow onion</td><td>30</td></tr>
<tr><td>2. Parsley</td><td>144</td><td>9. Violet cauliflower</td><td>9</td></tr>
<tr><td>3. White alyssum</td><td>128</td><td>10. Green cabbage</td><td>9</td></tr>
<tr><td>4. Cos lettuce</td><td>48</td><td>11. Carrot</td><td>72</td></tr>
<tr><td>5. Radish</td><td>48</td><td>12. Beet</td><td>18</td></tr>
<tr><td>6. Apricot alyssum</td><td>160</td><td>13. Red cabbage</td><td>9</td></tr>
<tr><td>7. Butterhead lettuce</td><td>56</td><td>14. Savoy cabbage</td><td>9</td></tr>
</table>

1 square = 1 ft.
Shaded areas are not planted.
Dots indicate stake placement for bed layout.

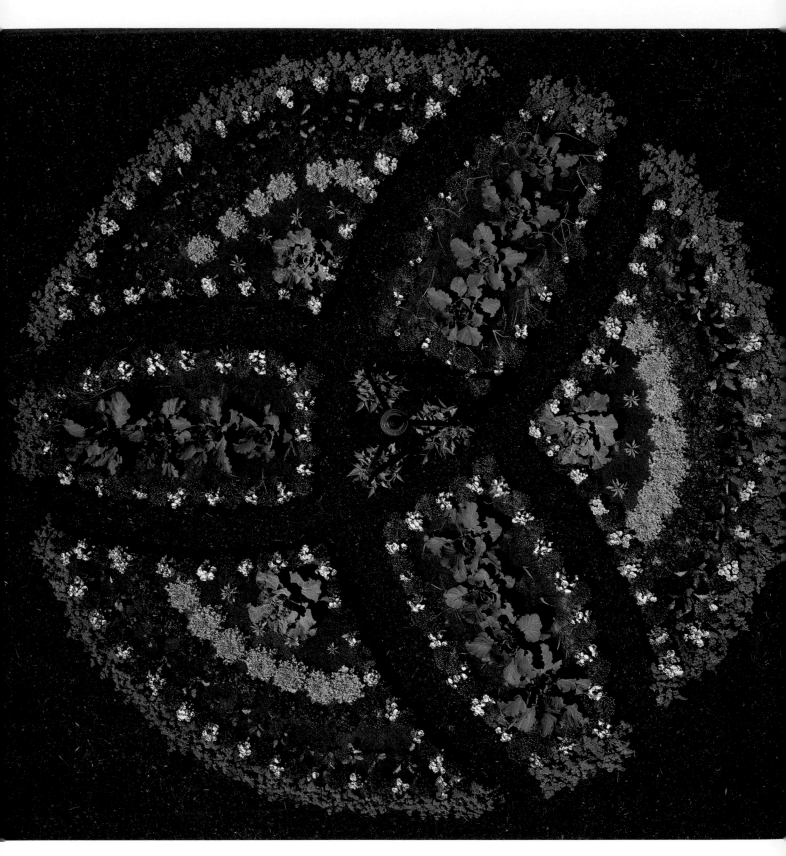

This garden, inspired by a Japanese family crest, is striking from any vantage point.

Japanese family crest

The graceful curves of a Japanese family crest inspired this circular garden (see the photo on the facing page). Three intersecting paths allowed easy access to the garden's interior. The resulting center point provided a perfect place for a vertical accent. We chose a beanpole tripod for the location, but a potted plant, a birdhouse, or a statue would also work. We embellished the borders with shades of deep blue and magenta lobelia and accented them with emerald-green parsley. Owing their graceful lines to the Japanese culture, these jewel-tone borders complemented the variety of vegetables in the beds (see the grid at right and the drawing and plant list on p. 60).

Grid for Japanese Family-Crest Garden

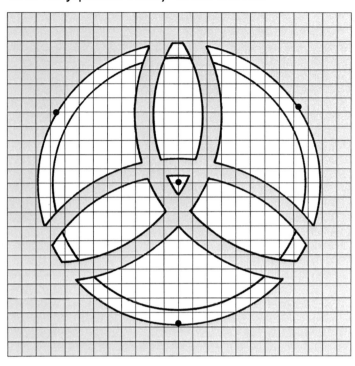

1 square = 1 ft.
Shaded areas are not planted.
Dots indicate stake placement for bed layout.

Jewel-tone borders of pansies and lobelia follow the graceful curves of this circular garden.

Japanese Family-Crest Garden

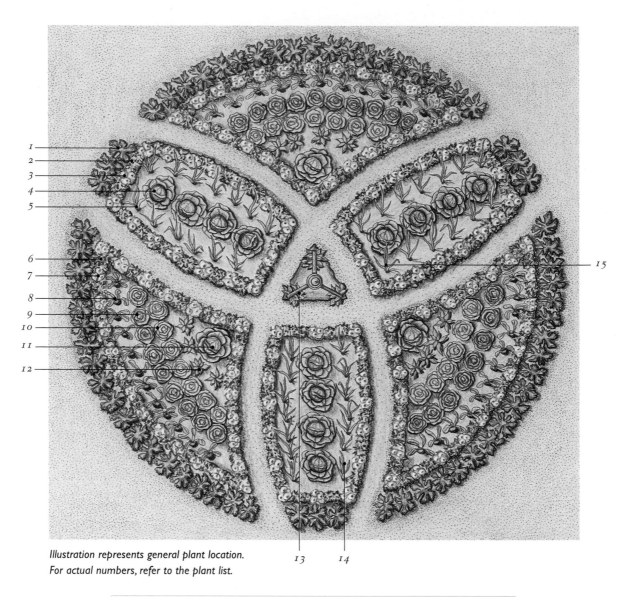

Illustration represents general plant location.
For actual numbers, refer to the plant list.

PLANT LIST

Plant	How many	Plant	How many
1. Parsley	108	*9.* Red-leaf lettuce	30
2. Magenta lobelia	63	*10.* Green oak-leaf lettuce	21
3. Magenta-faced pansy	63	*11.* Green cabbage	3
4. Red cabbage	12	*12.* Pepper	12
5. Red onion	30	*13.* Pole bean	9
6. Blue lobelia	93	*14.* Leek	30
7. Blue pansy	93	*15.* Yellow onion	30
8. Beet	48		

Celtic knot pattern

We used only a portion of a much-larger Celtic design to create the knot garden shown above. We interlaced ribbons of white and purple alyssum to form the knot.

To stake out and string the design, we used two colors of twine (on the grid on p. 62, the two different twine colors are indicated by solid and dashed lines). We assigned a particular plant color to each twine color. Weaving the strings over and under each other indicated which plant color needed to be "on top" at the intersecting points. At planting time, it was easy to set out the appropriate plants along the correct strings. By midsummer, the ribbons of flowers appeared woven together in a true Celtic knot (see the drawing and plant list on p. 63).

By midsummer, the lobelia completely filled in, creating an intense, solid-blue border.

Grid for Celtic Knot Garden

1 square = 1 ft.
Shaded areas are not planted.
Dots indicate stake placement
for bed layout.

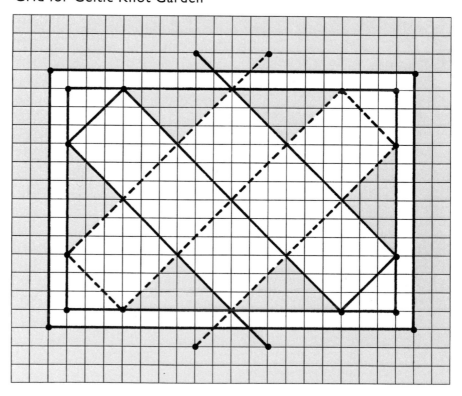

Celtic Knot Garden

Illustration represents general plant location.
For actual numbers, refer to the plant list.

PLANT LIST

Plant	How many	Plant	How many
1. Parsley	136	7. Beet	35
2. Blue lobelia	368	8. Red cabbage	9
3. Purple alyssum	114	9. Carrot	144
4. Red-leaf lettuce	16	10. Broccoli	9
5. Swiss chard	9	11. Yellow onion	36
6. White alyssum	114	12. Violet cauliflower	9

The Lobelia border around the perimeter of the garden is two rows wide. The rows are spaced 5 in. apart. Use 248 lobelia plugs for the border and split the remaining 120 plugs between the four corner triangles (30 plugs per triangle).

DESIGN DECISIONS

Before you begin drawing a new kitchen garden on paper, several important design decisions need to be made. These decisions will determine the location of your new garden, the types of plants and structures it will contain, the size of the beds within the garden's borders, and the size of paths. Once these determinations have been made, you can begin drawing the design on paper.

Location

The location of your garden will be your most important decision. Topography, soil, proximity to trees and structures, and viewpoint are all factors that need to be considered before you begin your design.

Your garden is comparable to an artist's canvas. Like a large painting, you will render your design on the soil surface. Your work of art will look best if it's grown on level ground; a hilly or uneven surface will

Gardens comprised of annuals and biodegradable paths can be totally turned under in the fall to clean the slate for a new design next season.

The rambling perennial berry vine in this bed is bordered by annual flowers: lobelia, alyssum, and pansies. (Technically perennials, we treat pansies as annuals.)

make the layout process difficult and will distort the final design.

Good soil is essential to a thriving and productive kitchen garden. If possible, locate your garden in an area of workable soil free of rocks and tree roots. Amending the soil with peat moss, manure, and compost will enhance the soil's fertility and improve its drainage.

Sunshine is an equally vital component in the production of healthy vegetable crops. If your prospective garden site is near trees or buildings, observe any shadows cast during the course of a day to make sure your garden will receive full sun.

For quick and handy harvesting, you may want your garden located near the kitchen. Freshly picked herbs and garnishes add a special touch to meals, but they may be dismissed if the garden is too far away.

A kitchen garden is enjoyed for its culinary contents as well as for its visual addition to the landscape. The colorful and elegantly shaped beds are wonderful to look at from any vantage point, but if you have a two-story house, the view from above is spectacular! Consider *all* viewing angles before you settle on your perfect garden location.

Once you've considered all the location requirements and have decided on an appropriate site for your kitchen garden, measure the available area to determine the maximum size of the garden. You will need an assistant, a measuring tape, a pencil, and paper to record the measurements.

Types of plants

Before you begin drawing the design, decide whether you would like an annual or perennial kitchen garden. Most vegetables are annuals (plants that complete their entire life cycle in one season). A garden composed entirely of annuals has its advantages; however, your kitchen garden may not be complete without a perennial patch of strawberries, a few clumps of chives, or a raspberry trellis.

The virtue of an annual garden is its versatility. If all the flowers, herbs, and vegetables are annuals and the paths are made from a biodegradable material, the entire garden can be turned under in the fall. If you have more than one design idea in mind, consider an annual garden. It's a wonderful way to try new garden configurations each year.

Some of the best kitchen gardens combine annuals and perennials to offer a full range of fruits, vegetables, herbs, and flowers. Segregating annuals and perennials in different

Trellises, fences, and an arbor add height to our kitchen garden.

A small bistro table offers a place to enjoy early morning coffee before a busy day.

beds will provide the greatest number of design options. For example, place perennials in the perimeter beds and annuals in the center beds. Mulch your paths with a biodegradable material. The center beds can then be totally turned under in the fall and a new design planted the following year, leaving the perennials untouched in the perimeter beds. You can still incorporate annual vegetables and annual flower borders in the perennial beds, but not the reverse.

Structures

We recommend using low-growing plants to create beautiful ornamental kitchen-garden patterns. Garden features and architectural structures add an important element of height to these otherwise low-lying landscapes. Like perennial and annual plants, garden structures can either be permanent or temporary.

In a small garden, a permanent structure may simply be the addition of a trellis. However, in medium-size and large gardens, permanent garden architecture can include fences, trellises, arbors, fountains, compost bins, cold frames, a tool shed, or a gazebo. The placement of large permanent structures needs to be carefully considered. They should blend in gracefully with your overall garden design and be positioned strategically to avoid casting unwanted shadows on the surrounding beds.

Temporary features include containers, outdoor furniture, freestanding trellises, potted topiaries, and statues. Although it is best to have a designated spot for these features, they can be spontaneously moved about the garden as situations and seasons change. For example, outdoor furniture can be moved in and out of the garden as the need arises as long as a large enough space was

In this bed, fresh butterhead lettuce is only an arm's reach away.

A stepping stone (one of three) provides easy access for blueberry picking in this large bed.

planned for it in the original design. Other temporary features include large containers that add height and a touch of formality to a garden. A neatly pruned bay tree or topiary standard planted in a large, decorative container, for instance, gives your garden a hint of old European kitchen-garden grace and grandeur. A small garden also benefits from the addition of several temporary features. Place a pot of flowers in the center of a small raised bed to add height or place four small topiary standards at the corners to add formality and charm.

Pay attention to detail as you choose your garden structures and features. Whether they are casual or formal, they need to be in proportion with the size of your garden and blend with the color and mood of your design. Selecting well-made structures and keeping them neatly maintained will add years to their life and volumes of classical distinction to your landscape.

Beds

A charming, easy-to-maintain kitchen garden is the result of carefully balancing small-scale vegetable production with an elegant garden presentation. To achieve this balance, beds must be small enough to be manageable yet large enough to be practical. In addition, the entire design must be proportionately pleasing.

For easy maintenance, the center of each bed should be within arm's reach. Generally, a bed (which can be accessed from all sides) should be no larger than 5 ft. across for comfortable weeding, watering, and harvesting. If intensively planted, it will generate an amazing amount of pro-

duce. A bed larger than 5 ft. across will require you to step into it for harvesting and maintenance. This can compact the soil too much over time. As a solution, consider the use of small stepping stones placed within the bed to localize the impact.

Paths

There is a trade-off between the use of paths as necessary delineations between garden beds and the amount of growing area they monopolize. As you design your garden on paper, vary the path widths to find the balance between form and function.

Paths are not necessary in a small garden because all areas are easily accessible. Medium-size and large gardens, however, require a network of paths or stepping pads to allow access to the garden's interior beds.

Use narrow paths or small stepping pads in a medium-size garden. For example, the paths of a 20-ft. by 20-ft. garden could be a mere 18 in. wide, which is wide enough for walking but too narrow for the passage of a wheelbarrow. Fortunately, a garden of this size is small enough that a wheelbarrow left at the garden's perimeter is never too far away. Small

Mulched stepping pads are integral to this Celtic design and allow access to the garden's interior beds. A basket can be used for weeding and harvesting.

baskets can be used for weeding and harvesting and then carried to the wheelbarrow. Stepping pads are used in a similar way. They are large enough to walk on, but they do not allow for wheelbarrow access.

A large garden may require paths at least 36 in. wide to accommodate the width of a wheelbarrow or a garden cart. A wheelbarrow left at the perimeter of a large garden is too far away to be practical. The best use of space in a large garden is a combination of wide and narrow paths. One or two wide paths intersecting the garden provide easy access, while

smaller walking paths can artistically delineate the perimeter beds.

As you determine the best dimensions for your paths, take into account the spreading growth habit of the border flowers. By midsummer, the flowers will consume several inches of space on both sides of the path. These flowers can be neatly trimmed back with a pair of grass clippers, but a portion of them should spill onto the paths to soften the lines and to add an element of charm.

In a large garden, fall cleanup is easy if the paths are wide enough to accommodate a wheelbarrow or garden cart.

Occasionally trim the flower borders to keep the paths and stepping pads clear.

MATERIALS LIST

- Tracing paper
- ¼-in. graph paper
- Compass (if any element of your design is circular)
- Pencil
- Ink pen or technical pen
- Eraser
- Ruler
- Measurements of your garden site
- Measurements of your garden structures
- Any inspirational objects, drawings, or photos

DRAWING YOUR KITCHEN-GARDEN DESIGN

With a basic plan in mind and after taking all necessary measurements outside, you can begin to make a scale drawing of your garden plan. Making a scale drawing is not difficult to do, but you'll need a few simple drawing tools (see the materials list at left).

Scale

The first step is deciding on the scale. Depending on the size of your garden and the size of your graph paper, determine a measurement for each square on the paper. For example, if you have ¼-in. graph paper, one ¼-in. square could equal 1 ft. of garden space (depending on the overall size of your garden). This measurement will keep your drawing to scale so it will correctly transfer to the garden site.

Initial layout

After deciding on the scale, begin the initial layout. On the graph paper, use your site measurements to pencil in dots around the garden perimeter. Use four dots—one at each corner—if your garden will be square or rectangular, or pencil in several dots around the perimeter if your garden will be circular or an irregular shape. These dots indicate the boundary lines of your garden.

Use tracing paper to sketch and doodle the first draft of your garden design.

Place tracing paper on top of the graph paper and sketch your preliminary garden design on the tracing paper. You can draw, doodle, and erase on the tracing paper without ruining the graph paper (see the bottom photo on the facing page).

It may be helpful to cut out the shapes of your preliminary bed designs from a separate piece of paper and move them around on the grid until the configuration is proportionally pleasing (see the photo at right). Check the path and bed widths for maneuverability and pencil in the dimensions of your garden structures. Continue reworking your design until you are satisfied.

The final design

Once you have finished your design, place the graph paper on top of the tracing paper and transfer the design to the graph paper using a pencil. Finish the plan by using a pen and ruler (or compass) to ink in the final drawing over the penciled lines (see the photo at right). Place dots at all the points requiring stakes necessary to string out the design in the garden.

This graph-paper drawing is your master plan. When it's complete, you are ready to select the flowers and vegetables that will flourish in your new kitchen garden. In the following chapter, you will use the drawing to determine the number of plants you will need and where they will be located within your garden beds.

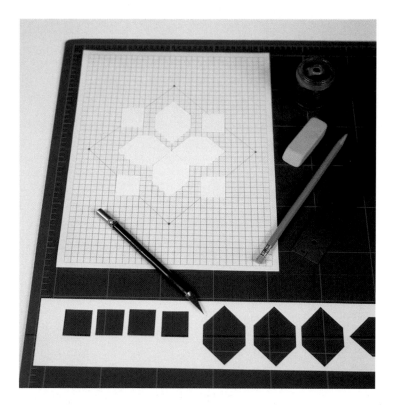

Cut out garden-bed shapes and move them around on the grid to create a pleasing overall design.

Ink in your final design on the graph paper.

Flowers and vegetables offer a multitude of colors, textures, and heights for a kitchen gardener.

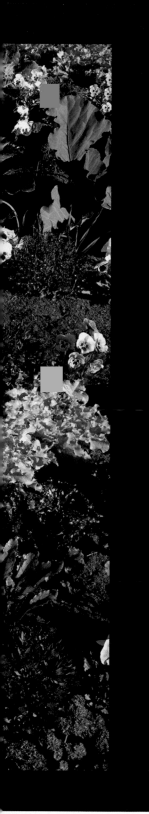

chapter three

Plant Selection

*f*rom an artistic point of view, plants are a marvelous medium to work in because they offer a multitude of colors, textures, and heights.

Creating a garden design with a diverse group of plants is both challenging and rewarding. For kitchen gardeners, an added benefit is that the various plants you incorporate into your landscape also carry into your kitchen. Appealing and delicious meals can be created when you have an assortment of vegetables from which to choose.

In this chapter, we'll explain how to mix colors, add texture, and combine plant heights to create a harmonious design. Once you understand these concepts, you'll be able to compile a list of plants and add them to your graph-paper plan (see Chapter 2). By following these principles of design, you can achieve a unique and colorful kitchen garden.

MIXING COLORS

Color is the first design element you notice in the kitchen gardens presented in this book. It sets the mood, leads your eye, and defines the design. Garden colors come from a variety of sources, including flowers, fruits, vegetables, foliage, stems, landscape materials, garden structures, and accents, such as statues and containers.

Choosing a color scheme is a very personal choice. For instance, you may want to blend your kitchen-garden colors with those already present in your existing landscape, or you may want to coordinate them with the color of your home or a nearby garden structure or trellis.

Understanding the principles of color theory will help you make plant selections. Getting acquainted with the color wheel and the relationships between colors is the first step.

Color wheel

The color wheel is arranged into 12 equal sections, as shown on the facing page. Three sections comprise the primary colors: red, yellow, and blue. These colors cannot be achieved by mixing any other colors.

Centered between the primary colors are the secondary colors: green, orange, and violet. These colors are produced by mixing two primary colors together in approximately equal amounts: red and blue create violet, red and yellow produce orange, and yellow and blue make green.

The remaining six sections are the tertiary, or intermediate, colors: yellow-orange, yellow-green, blue-green, blue-violet, red-violet, and red-orange. They are obtained by mixing adjacent primary and secondary colors together. Depending on the proportions of each color being mixed, it's possible to achieve a near infinite spectrum of colors.

If we divide the color wheel in half between yellow-green and green, and red-violet and red, the left side represents *warm* colors and the right half *cool* colors.

The *value* of a color refers to its lightness or darkness, as shown at the bottom of the facing page. A color in its purest form is called a *hue*. A color darker than the pure hue contains black and is called a *shade*. A color lighter than the pure hue contains white and is called a *tint*. A color containing gray is called a *tone*.

How color affects your garden

Much to a gardener's delight (and sometimes bewilderment), a vast spectrum of hues, shades, tints, and tones can be found in plants. For example, warm colors, including amber, orange, chartreuse, and scarlet, can be found in Swiss chard, carrots, golden beets, lettuce, marigolds, and calendula. Colors in the cool range include lavender, purple, blue-green, and fuchsia, which can be found in plants such as red cabbage, broccoli, kohlrabi, pansies, and lobelia.

The use of warm and cool colors can affect the mood of your garden and even create the illusion of distance. For instance, warm colors

COLOR WHEEL

COOL COLORS

GREEN
YELLOW-GREEN
BLUE-GREEN
YELLOW
BLUE
YELLOW-ORANGE
BLUE-VIOLET
ORANGE
VIOLET
RED-ORANGE
RED-VIOLET
RED

WARM COLORS

COLOR VALUES

| HUE | SHADE | TINT | TONE |

This monochromatic white theme consists of white alyssum, dusty miller, and white Swiss chard.

design and up the matching purple beanpole tripod. The rows of red- and green-leaf lettuce and beets mimic the circular curves of the overall garden configuration.

Color schemes

As we said before, the color scheme for your new kitchen garden is a personal choice. Color combinations that appeal to some people will not please others. Knowing there is no right or wrong way to mix colors will free you to experiment. Whether you prefer an orderly placement of coordinated colors or a mixture of bright rainbow hues, the following standard ways to mix color can offer inspiration as you design your own custom color scheme.

Monochromatic

Monochromatic color schemes are based on one hue, including all of its gradations of shades, tints, and tones (see the photo at left). For example, a blue-violet theme might include values ranging from deep shades of plum, through indigo, and on into light tints of lavender. Of course, in a garden it's impossible to achieve a totally monochromatic scheme because of the green foliage (see the sidebar on p. 81). To keep these schemes from becoming monotonous, use a wide range of shades, tints, and tones within the color and work in various textures and heights.

Complementary

Complementary color schemes create contrast by combining colors that are directly opposite each other on the color wheel. For example, yellow contrasts with violet and blue contrasts with orange.

such as bright yellow or orange, are eye catching and stimulating. They dominate the scene, appearing to advance and visually come to the foreground. Cool colors, on the other hand, such as pale shades of blue, are calming, tranquil, and subtle and tend to recede visually.

Color is also used to define the patterns and lead the viewer's eye. Both flowers and vegetables can be used for this purpose. The garden design shown on p. 20 is a good example. The vibrant lobelia colors in that garden (inspired by a Japanese family crest) instantly define the garden pattern. Meanwhile, the bluish-purple cabbages and indigo lobelia lead your eye to the center of the

Buttermilk-yellow pansies subtly contrast with the light-violet alyssum in this complementary color scheme. The light, yellow-green leaves of lettuce coordinate nicely with the deep-green pansy leaves and the pale-yellow flowers.

Depending on the values of the colors used, the contrast can be either vivid or subtle. For example, the use of pale yellow and light violet gives a soft appearance (see the photo above), whereas a combination of bright orange and vibrant indigo is more exuberant (see the photo at right). Another way to combine contrasting colors is to use the strong hue of one color, such as deep purple, and a much lighter value of its contrasting color, light yellow.

To moderate bright color combinations in a complementary color scheme, add gray foliage plants, such as dusty miller.

Strong contrast is made with this complementary arrangement of bright-orange marigolds and deep-indigo lobelia. Notice how the ruffled texture of the red-leaf lettuce is repeated on a smaller scale in the marigold petals.

Harmonious

Harmonious color schemes are created by combining two or three analogous colors (see the photo below). These colors are directly next to each other on the color wheel—for instance, violet and blue-violet or orange, red-orange, and red. It's easy to create harmony with these color schemes because the colors are so closely related. Use gradations of color values from deep shades to light tints to energize these combinations.

Polychromatic

Polychromatic schemes use any or all of the colors in the spectrum. These multicolored combinations can be bright, exciting mixtures of intense hues or subtle combinations of pale pastels. Random placement of color often reveals some unexpectedly pleasing combinations (keep notes on these unforeseen triumphs so they can be reproduced in future designs).

Keep in mind, the use of bright, multicolored schemes can look busy and chaotic in the enclosed space of a small garden. Use white flowers or silvery-gray foliage plants to help temper and separate clashing colors.

How to coordinate plant colors

Once you have a basic color scheme in mind, you can use it to help determine which flowers and vegetables will fit into your plan. To help us coordinate the colors in our gardens, we cut out pictures from old seed catalogs (being careful to preserve the plant's name accompanying the

Indigo lobelia and violet alyssum combine to make this harmonious arrangement. The veins of the red-cabbage leaves coordinate with the alyssum, while the blue-green background keeps this entire grouping in the cool range.

This monochromatic magenta arrangement encompasses a range of shades and tints. Because some of the pansy tints are so light, the white pansies blend in harmoniously. Adding to the harmony are the similar textures of the ruffled cabbage leaves and pansy petals.

Using White and Green in the Garden

White and green are used in several ways in garden color schemes. White objects reflect all wavelengths of light. Like black and grays, white has no color of its own (achromatic) and therefore blends easily with either warm or cool colors. When white is placed in a color scheme containing tints, it blends harmoniously. However, it creates a sharp contrast when it's paired with bright hues and deep shades. Both white and gray can be used to buffer clashing colors.

Because green is an inherent color in gardens (especially in vegetable gardens), you need to consider its range of colors and values. Green provides a backdrop for the colorful vegetables and flowers. Yet on its own, green has many gradations. Vegetable greens can run the gamut from the cool, subdued blue-green of broccoli to the warm, bright yellow-green of 'Salad Bowl' leaf lettuce. This assortment allows you to choose the perfect greens to complement your color scheme.

White creates a stark contrast when combined with deep shades and bright hues.

Even root crops can add a touch of color. Here, red-beet stems blend beautifully with red-tinged lettuce.

photo). We placed these photos on a table and arranged them until we found pleasing combinations. Sometimes the colors reproduced in catalogs are not identical to the actual flowers and vegetables, but they are usually good enough to help you visualize your chosen color scheme. Experience is the best teacher, so experiment and have fun with color. Working with annual flowers and vegetables affords you the flexibility of changing your color scheme each year.

Although root crops add only a bit of color, they too can contribute to

the design. Beets are the best example (see the photo above): Both the red and golden varieties have beautifully colored stems. And even though your orange carrots won't be visible, their feathery foliage will add texture and a bright, emerald-green hue to your color scheme.

Coordinating colors in your kitchen garden may introduce you to new varieties. For instance, if your color scheme includes shades of violet and your family enjoys peppers, beans, or kohlrabi, try growing the purple varieties of these vegetables. Remember that color coordination is important but not at the expense of leaving out some of your favorite vegetables. Let the majority of color come from the decorative borders, landscape materials, and structures, and where possible, include pleasing combinations of coordinated vegetable colors.

ADDING TEXTURE

As you select plants for your garden, think about the myriad textures that exist and how they might be combined to create textural tapestries. Vegetables, flowers, fruits, and stems

Use vegetables, flowers, fruits, stems, and foliage to create textural tapestries.

Texture is an important design element in a garden with low-growing plants. Here, the fernlike foliage of marigolds borders the broad leaves of radicchio, which ring a ruffled center display of green oak-leaf lettuce.

This monochromatic color scheme of yellow sunflowers, yellow marigolds, and yellow bush beans is made interesting through the contrasting textures of the leaves, flowers, and pods.

This harmonious pairing of young dill plants and ornamental kale also exhibits a good mix of leaf textures.

all contribute texture to a garden scene, but foliage is the main source. Leaf textures can be large, bold, and architectural like those of rhubarb and artichokes or small, delicate, and feathery like those of dill and carrots. In many kitchen-garden designs, where the majority of plants are low growing and there is little variance in height, variations in texture become increasingly important to add interest (see the top photo on the facing page).

The use of contrasting textures is the best way to create interest. For example, group plants with varying leaf sizes and shapes (see the bottom photos on the facing page). You might border large-leaf squash plants with the delicate, fernlike foliage of marigolds or combine the feathery plumes of dill with the large, serrated leaves of ornamental kale.

From the dainty cushions of alyssum to the ruffled spheres of marigolds, flowers also add texture to your garden. Varieties that bloom throughout the summer offer continuous texture and color. Consider the fuzzy, pufflike blooms of ageratum, the small, starry flowers of phlox, or the delicate, petite blossoms of lobelia. Beautiful arrangements can be designed by using similar textures on different scales. For instance, you could pair large, ruffled cabbage leaves and the smaller ruffled petals of pansies (see the top photo on p. 81).

While fruits and vegetables do add texture (like the nubby heads of cauliflower and broccoli), their presence is fleeting due to harvesting. It's best to rely on their foliage to contribute texture to the garden design.

At the heart of artful kitchen-garden designs are small, compact flowers and vegetables.

COMBINING HEIGHTS

Along with color and texture, the height of plants plays an important role in kitchen-garden design. To achieve balance, plant combinations must be proportionate to each other as well as to the area in which they are planted. As with color and texture, it's also important to vary plant heights so that the design does not become monotonous.

Where to place small, compact plants

Small, compact flowers and vegetables (6 in. to 12 in. high) are at the core of the garden designs in this book. Most often they are used as borders, edgings, or ground covers, and when planted in patterns, they resemble ornate tapestries.

Use bold, medium-size plants to create focal points in the garden.

The borders in our gardens are comprised of short, compact flowers and foliage plants that provide continuous color throughout the summer. Foliage plants such as bright-green parsley, silvery-gray dusty miller, and even red- and green-leaf lettuce make attractive—and sometimes edible—edgings. Vibrant flowers such as lobelia, pansies, and phlox bloom steadily and delineate garden patterns vividly.

Small, compact plants can create a solid carpet effect within the borders of beds. For instance, endive, lettuce, lobelia, or alyssum will completely fill in beds until the soil disappears from view. It's particularly important to use short, compact plants around stepping pads so that it's easy to stride into the garden without obstruction.

Place tall plants in island beds to avoid breaking up your design or casting shadows on surrounding plants.

Where to place medium-size plants

In our kitchen gardens, which are essentially comprised of low-growing plants, medium-size plants (12 in. to 24 in. high) offer height and structure, but not to the extent that they break up the design.

Medium-size vegetables come in an array of colors, textures, and bold shapes. If you group them in the center of a design, they make a striking focal point that is slightly elevated above the surrounding, low-growing vegetables and flower borders. Consider the bold blue-green foliage of broccoli and cabbages, the striking ruby stems of Swiss chard, or the vivid hue of purple kohlrabi. Any one of these beautiful vegetables is worthy of a central placement. Medium-size vegetables with smaller leaves or less form, such as bush beans or potatoes, can be used as fillers in surrounding beds.

Perimeter beds are perfect areas for tall plants such as this blueberry bush.

plants, if positioned incorrectly, can break up the harmony of a pattern created by the lower-growing plants.

As you design your garden, place tall plants in specific areas. Small "island" beds are perfect for tall plants. The beds are part of the overall design, yet they are isolated so shadows cast by the towering plants will fall on the paths, not on the surrounding beds. Perimeter beds are another good place for tall plants, leaving the center of the garden open for a low-growing pattern design. The perimeter corners are particularly well suited for tall accents such as a group of rhubarb, asparagus, or a blueberry bush. A single, tall specimen, like a bold-leaf cardoon or artichoke, would make an impressive silvery-green centerpiece in a small garden.

Corn is the one tall vegetable that is difficult to incorporate into relatively small, design-oriented gardens. Corn must be grown in groups or in side-by-side rows for pollination, making artistic arrangements difficult. But if you're like us, summer just isn't complete without fresh, homegrown corn. So we suggest you grow this tall crop in a separate area of your yard or grow it in rows on the north side of your garden as a backdrop. If you have a large kitchen garden, consider growing corn in island beds.

The long, swordlike silhouettes of onions, garlic, and leeks add height and a wonderful contrast to bushy, leafy greens. For an interesting blend, try grouping these slender vegetables with a delicate, low-growing flower border and a background of taller, bold-leaf vegetables, such as cabbage and kale.

Where to place tall plants

Tall plants (24 in. to 36 in. high) provide important vertical accents in kitchen gardens. If positioned carefully among the small and medium-size plants, they can become focal points, adding height and structure to the design. But beware. Tall

Where to place vines

Vines also can be used to add height to kitchen gardens. The graceful curves of their twining stems and curly tendrils add interest and contrast to the straight lines of low-growing geometric beds. Vines also excel at softening the hard lines of fences and trellises.

*Vines are excellent for softening the hard
lines of fences and trellises.*

A beanpole tripod adds color and height and also becomes a focal point in the garden.

Create a garden room by training vines on perimeter fences.

Most vines will gladly climb up a support, where they often become a focal point in the garden. For instance, a decorative beanpole tripod positioned in the center of a garden design will add height, structure, and a beautiful leafy display. Peas, cucumbers, and squash will create an enclosed "garden room" if they are grown up a perimeter fence.

If vines are left to trail on the ground, they tend to take over and can be a bit tricky to control in a small, geometric garden bed. Squash, for instance, will create a marvelous leafy ground cover; however, you will need to reposition these vigorous vines every few days to keep them growing within the borders. If the vines get too long, they may need a light trim. A little rearranging and light trimming won't hurt these

Colors, Textures, and Heights of Vegetables & Fruits

	Leaf: Green	Leaf: Blue-green	Leaf: Red and green	Leaf: Yellow-green	Stem: White	Stem: Green	Stem: Purple	Stem: Red	Stem: Yellow	Veg/Fruit: White	Veg/Fruit: Green	Veg/Fruit: Blue-green	Veg/Fruit: Blue	Veg/Fruit: Purple	Veg/Fruit: Red	Veg/Fruit: Red-orange	Veg/Fruit: Orange	Veg/Fruit: Yellow	Flowers: White	Flowers: Purple	Flowers: Red	Flowers: Yellow	Architectural	Feathery	Swordlike	Ruffled	Bold	Finely cut	Serrated	Leafy	6 in.–12 in.	12 in.–24 in.	24 in.–36 in.	36 in. and taller
Artichoke		●									●									●			●				●							●
Asparagus	●									●														●										●
Bean (bush/vine)	●					●	●			●		●							●	●	●									●		●		●
Beet	●		●			●		●	●																		●			●	●			
Blueberry	●											●	●						●											●				●
Broccoli		●									●																●					●		
Brussel sprout	●					●					●																●						●	
Cabbage		●																																
Cardoon		●									●									●			●											●
Carrot	●																							●							●			
Cauliflower	●					●				●				●													●				●			
Collard	●																										●			●			●	
Cucumber	●					●					●							●									●			●				
Eggplant	●						●				●			●						●							●			●		●		
Endive	●			●																						●					●			
Kale		●																								●	●				●			
Kohlrabi	●				●		●				●															●	●					●		
Leek		●																							●							●		
Lettuce	●		●	●																										●	●			
Okra	●					●		●			●			●																●				●
Onion		●																							●							●		
Parsnip	●																													●		●		
Pea	●										●								●											●				●
Pepper	●					●					●				●		●	●	●											●		●		
Potato	●					●														●										●		●		
Radish	●																													●	●			
Raspberry	●														●															●				●
Rhubarb	●							●															●				●						●	
Rutabaga	●																										●			●		●		
Spinach	●																													●	●			
Squash	●					●	●	●		●							●	●				●					●						●	●
Swiss chard	●		●		●			●																			●			●		●		
Tomato	●					●									●	●	●	●				●								●			●	●
Turnip	●																										●			●		●		

plants, but to be fair, only grow squash vines in beds where they can stretch out a good 5 ft. to 6 ft.

ARRANGING PLANTS

Now it's time to work through the puzzle of compiling your plant list and coordinating their colors, textures, and heights. (If you want to extend your harvest with succession planting or interplanting, these crops should also be coordinated at this time. We'll discuss succession planting and interplanting in Chapter 4.)

Begin by making a list of the vegetables your family enjoys. These plants will comprise the majority of vegetables in your garden. Each year, experiment with a few new selections. Who knows, your list of family favorites may increase! While searching for plants to use in the cool side of our large feature garden (see p. 38), we chose purple kohlrabi because of its striking color, blue-green foliage, and interesting shape. Our search for an aesthetically beautiful plant variety introduced us to a delicious new vegetable.

If your design begs for red cabbage, yet no one in your family eats it, don't despair. Vegetables can be viewed like flowers—integral elements of a design but not necessarily edible. At harvest time, share these homegrown gifts with "gardenless" friends and neighbors or with your local food bank.

The same is true of the quantity you grow. A case in point is parsley. We like to use parsley as a lush, emerald-green border. Although we cook with both fresh and dried parsley, our harvesting doesn't put a dent in the amount we grow. Yet we feel our designs just wouldn't be the same without the use of parsley borders. Lettuce, when planted in large quantities to create borders and carpet effects, can also leave you with an overabundance. But again, lettuce can be viewed as an ornamental plant, and because it is fast and easy to grow, we feel our time has not been wasted if we don't eat every head. To extend the life of your design using lettuce, stagger the sowing times (see p. 100) and plant the younger and older seedlings side by side in an alternating pattern along the borders or within the beds.

Carefully combining the colors, textures, and heights of your chosen plants will keep your design visible throughout the season. Again, be aware that some plants can obscure your design: Sprawling vines can outgrow their borders and blur the pattern, tall plants can break it up, and whole border designs can be lost if they are planted with flowers that only bloom for short a period of time.

To work out the placement of your chosen plants, place a sheet of tracing paper over your inked graph-paper plan (see Chapter 2). Block in

Colors, Textures, and Heights of Border Flowers

	White	Silvery-gray	Green	Blue-violet	Lavender	Violet-purple	Magenta	Rose	Pink	Red	Red-orange	Orange	Yellow-orange	Yellow	Yellow-green	Curly	Finely cut	Fernlike	Pointed	Ruffled	Dainty	Flat/round	Ruffled	Spherical	Daisylike	Roselike	Starry	Fuzzy	Feathery	Cushion	Mound	Bushy	3 in.–6 in.	6 in.–12 in.
	FLOWER OR FOLIAGE COLOR															*Foliage*					*Flowers*									*Form*			**HEIGHT**	
Ageratum	●			●	●	●		●																				●				●	●	
Alyssum	●				●			●						●							●									●			●	
Calendula												●	●	●											●							●		●
Celosia							●	●	●	●	●	●	●	●														●	●			●		●
Chives								●										●			●			●										●
Dianthus	●						●	●	●	●												●										●		●
Dusty miller		●															●																	●
Fibrous begonia	●							●	●													●											●	
Lettuce			●							●					●					●													●	
Lobelia	●			●	●	●															●												●	
Marigold											●	●	●	●			●						●	●								●		●
Nierembergia	●				●																							●			●		●	
Cabbage/kale	●					●	●														●													●
Pansy/viola	●			●	●	●	●	●	●	●		●		●								●	●										●	
Parsley			●													●																		●
Phlox	●			●			●	●	●												●											●	●	
Portulaca	●						●	●	●				●													●					●		●	
Verbena	●					●	●	●	●																			●				●	●	
Zinnia	●							●	●	●		●		●											●							●		●

your preliminary plant selections by shading the general areas where the plants will be located. Use colored pencils or markers to help coordinate colors. For reference, use the charts on p. 91 and above, which indicate the colors, textures, and heights of some vegetables and flowers suitable for kitchen gardens. For plants not listed here or for more information, consult your seed catalogs.

Determining the number of plants

Once you've blocked in your general plant placements on the tracing-paper overlay, count the individual plants. For reference, use the spacing guides on p. 94. However, plant sizes vary with each variety, so use your seed catalogs for specific sizes and spacing requirements.

Count the individual squares on your graph-paper plan to determine the dimensions of each bed. Use

Vegetable Spacing Guide

VEGETABLE	SPACING	VEGETABLE	SPACING
Artichoke	24 in. - 36 in.	Leek	6 in.
Basil	6 in. - 8 in.	Lettuce	10 in.
Bean	6 in. - 8 in.	Okra	16 in. - 18 in.
Beet	4 in. - 6 in.	Onion	4 in. - 6 in.
Broccoli	12 in. - 18 in.	Parsnip	6 in. - 8 in.
Brussel sprout	12 in. - 18 in.	Pea	3 in.
Cabbage	12 in. - 18 in.	Pepper	15 in.
Cardoon	24 in. - 36 in.	Potato	12 in.
Carrot	2 in. - 3 in.	Radish	2 in. - 3 in.
Cauliflower	12 in. - 18 in.	Rhubarb	36 in.
Collard	10 in. - 12 in.	Rutabaga	6 in. - 8 in.
Cucumber	12 in.	Spinach	6 in.
Eggplant	16 in. - 18 in.	Squash	18 in. - 24 in.
Endive	10 in. - 12 in.	Swiss chard	10 in. - 12 in.
Kale	12 in. - 16 in.	Tomato	18 in. - 24 in.
Kohlrabi	6 in. - 8 in.	Turnip	4 in. - 6 in.

Flower Spacing Guide

FLOWER	SPACING	FLOWER	SPACING
Ageratum	6 in. - 8 in.	Marigold	6 in. - 12 in.
Alyssum	6 in. - 8 in.	Nierembergia	8 in. - 12 in.
Calendula	8 in.	Cabbage/kale	10 in. - 12 in.
Celosia	8 in. - 12 in.	Pansy/viola	6 in. - 8 in.
Chive	6 in. - 8 in.	Parsley	6 in. - 8 in.
Dianthus	6 in. - 8 in.	Phlox	6 in.
Dusty miller	6 in. - 8 in.	Portulaca	6 in. - 12 in.
Fibrous begonia	6 in. - 12 in.	Verbena	6 in. - 12 in.
Lettuce	10 in.	Zinnia	6 in. - 8 in.
Lobelia	4 in. - 6 in.		

those dimensions to calculate how many plants you will need for each area in your garden. For example, say one square on your graph paper equals 1 ft. If your bed is 5 ft. by 5 ft., you could grow nine broccoli plants in the center spaced 12 in. apart (see the sample grid at right). Ringing the broccoli could be a row of alternating beets (16) and onions (16) spaced every 6 in., bordered by a perimeter planting of 40 lobelia plugs also spaced 6 in. apart. With this configuration, the lobelia, planted directly next to the perimeter of the bed, will spill onto the path a good 3 in. Take this into consideration if your path widths are narrow. Depending on the size of your garden, you can draw the individual plants right onto your graph-paper plan for reference.

The number of plants you calculate will be approximate, especially for the border plants. For example, we wanted the ribbons of alyssum that formed the knot pattern in our Celtic garden (see p. 63) to fill in quickly, so we spaced them closer than normally recommended. If you prefer to use fewer plants, they will fill in, but it will take longer. (When choosing your border plants, select varieties that remain under 12 in.)

Always plant more than you think you will need. Fluctuations in germi-

Sample Grid for Plant Spacing

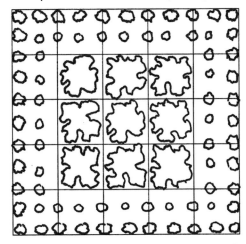

I square = I ft.

nation rates and seedlings lost to pests or unexpected disasters may lower your seedling count by planting time. We even keep a few extra seedlings growing in our cold frames until we're sure the seedlings planted in the garden are doing well. One year an opportunistic deer came through our gardens for a midnight snack. In the morning we were able to replace the chewed off vegetables with like-size plants from the cold frame, allowing the design to grow on uninterrupted.

Starting your own seeds and transplanting them to the garden is relatively easy and very rewarding.

chapter four

Growing Basics

*M*ost annual flowers and vegetables are easily grown from seed. Once you learn the growing techniques, a world of gardening possibilities awaits you. Seed catalogs are full of beautiful flowers and a wide variety of vegetables, many of which cannot be found at local garden centers.

Whether you are growing just a few plants for a window box or enough to fill a large garden, the process is basically the same. You simply need the space and time to do it. If space and time are in short supply, purchasing some or all of your seedlings from a nursery may be your best option. Regardless of whether you grow your own seeds or buy seedlings, in this chapter we'll show you how to obtain the plants for your new kitchen garden.

GROWING FROM SEED

The medium-size and large gardens presented in this book require substantial quantities of plants to create the decorative borders. We realize that the thought of starting 145 parsley plants or 250 pansies may at first seem daunting, but the process is actually quite simple and, in the end, very rewarding.

Growing your own plants from seed has many benefits. The primary advantage is the money you'll save. An inexpensive packet of seeds and a bag of soil mix will produce a flat (or tray) of plants at a fraction of the cost of buying the same number of plants at a nursery. Selection is also increased when you grow your own seedlings. For example, some seed catalogs carry upwards of 45 varieties of lettuce, allowing you to choose just the right color, texture, and taste. Your local nursery may not carry such an extensive inventory. Also, by growing your own seedlings, you can control the planting schedule so that your vegetables mature at the proper times, allowing you to grow successive crops and extend your harvest.

We suggest you start the majority of your seeds indoors in flats or other containers and transplant them to the garden when they are seedlings. Seeds planted in the garden are faced with fluctuations in moisture and temperature and the possibility of being eaten by birds or rodents. This often results in uneven germination rates and gaps in the garden design. (Two vegetables we do suggest you sow directly in the garden are radishes and carrots.) Another ad-

vantage of growing indoors and transplanting is that you have more control over plant spacing and placement, which is especially important when creating geometric designs.

The transformation from a tiny seed to a leafy plant will only occur if you provide the proper growing conditions. Planting times, space, light, temperature, and moisture all need to be considered to ensure successful germination and plant growth.

When to plant seeds

By late February, spring fever has infected most gardeners. After a few sunny days, enthusiastic gardeners (ourselves included!) are convinced spring is here to stay. But in many regions, Mother Nature will have a few more surprises for us before she delivers consistent mild weather. Resist the urge to start your seeds too early because the resulting seedlings may be ready to transplant to the garden while there is still a danger of frost. Seedlings transplanted to the garden in mild conditions usually catch up to those that were transplanted several weeks prior and had to struggle through cold snaps.

Before you plant, consider the timing of your harvest and the amount of vegetables you want your garden to produce. Many gardeners enjoy the excitement of starting seeds in spring, nurturing the plants through the summer, reaping the harvest, and calling it a season. Others prefer to grow a succession of crops throughout the spring, summer, and fall to maximize the varieties and quantities of vegetables in their gardens. In either case, if you're sowing seeds, timing is everything.

Sample Spring Planting Schedule

MARCH				APRIL				MAY			
Dates for starting seeds indoors								Transplant into garden			
1 - 7	8 - 15	16 - 22	23 - 31	1 - 7	8 - 15	16 - 22	23 - 30	1 - 7	8 - 15	16 - 22	23 - 31
Leek Lobelia	Cardoon Pansy	Eggplant Parsley Pepper Tomato		Broccoli Cabbage Cauliflower Kale	Endive Kohlrabi	Alyssum Calendula Marigold	Beet Cucumber Lettuce Spinach Summer squash Sunflower Swiss chard	Broccoli Cabbage Cauliflower Kale Leek Parsley	Alyssum Beet Calendula Cardoon Endive Pansy Kohlrabi Lettuce Lobelia Marigold Spinach Sunflower Swiss chard	Cucumber Eggplant Pepper Summer squash Tomato	

Our last frost date is May 10.

Creating a spring planting schedule
To create wonderful designs with plants, timing your seedling production is very important. All of your border plants and the majority of your vegetables need to be transplanted into the garden at approximately the same time. This produces a "peak" display in about 10 to 12 weeks from transplanting them into the garden.

We generally use the first three weeks of May to transplant our seedlings into the garden. We put in the cool-season plants, such as kale, leek, and broccoli, during the first week of May. The majority of flowers and vegetables go in around mid-May, and we finish with tomatoes, eggplants, squash, and peppers in the third week of the month or when nighttime temperatures have moderated. If necessary, we protect individual tender plants at night with a simple cloche (see pp. 111 and 114).

To plan your spring seeding schedule you will need a calendar, your seed packets (and/or seed catalogs), and the average date of your region's last spring frost (this information is available through your county's Co-operative Extension Agent).

Many seed packets and catalogs give instructions for starting seeds early. For instance, the directions might read, "Start cabbage seeds indoors, four to six weeks prior to the last hard frost." Plan your planting schedule from this information. On your calendar, mark the average date of your region's last spring frost. Then count the weeks backward from that date and write in the names of the plants to be started during those weeks. Unfortunately, this is not an exacting science due to varying germination rates and environmental factors. By keeping records from year to year of your sowing, transplanting, and harvesting

*Growing successive
crops in a kitchen-
garden design
requires timing
and aesthetic
consideration.*

times, you can fine-tune your schedule for the future. A sample of our spring planting schedule is shown on p. 99.

Creating a successive-crop schedule
Creating a successive-crop schedule is fairly straightforward for vegetable gardeners planting in rows, but it requires a bit more thought for an aesthetically minded kitchen gardener. You must coordinate short- and long-season crops, as well as the arrangement of plant colors, textures, and heights. Lest you be dissuaded, consider the benefits: In a small garden, techniques such as staggering sowing times, interplanting, and successive planting utilize the land to its fullest, keeping a continuous supply of fresh

vegetables on your table and extending the life of your garden design.

These intensive planting methods require fertile soil. Amend your garden in the spring and apply additional organic fertilizers as necessary throughout the growing season. To keep the pattern of your design consistent, sow the seeds for your border plants (parsley, pansies, alyssum, etc.) at their proper times in the spring and use the following planting methods to create successive vegetable crops within the borders.

Staggering sowing times—The easiest way to grow a continuous supply of vegetables is by staggering the sowing times. Starting at the recommended sowing date in the spring, simply plant small amounts of the same seeds at 10- to 14-day intervals. Use this technique for small-leaf vegetables (spinach, carrots, beets, radishes, etc.) that serve as fillers in your design, not focal points. The varying height differences are not as noticeable with small plants.

Staggering sowing times extends your harvest over several weeks so you're not deluged with any one vegetable. Also, by randomly planting the different-age seedlings across the bed, the subsequent random harvesting will reduce large bare spots in your garden design. (If you are sowing seeds directly into the garden, such as those for carrots and radishes, randomly scatter and cover small amounts of seed over the bed at 10- to 14-day intervals and thin as necessary.) Unlike interplanting and succession planting, the same vegetables are used throughout the growing season, eliminating the need to incorporate new varieties into your design.

Interplanting—Interplanting, or intercropping, is the method of planting fast- and slow-growing crops side by side. Each has a different

Four cabbages and six heads of lettuce were interplanted in this small raised bed. When the lettuce matured, it was harvested, leaving plenty of room for the developing cabbages.

maturing rate, so fast-growing crops are harvested and removed, making room for slower-growing plants. Radishes, lettuce, and cabbages make an excellent mix for interplanting. The small radishes are harvested first, maturing in only 25 days, followed by medium-size lettuce, which matures in 55 days. Both the radishes and lettuce are gone before the larger, slower-growing cabbages need all the space. The varying textures and heights of these plants create an aesthetically pleasing arrangement.

Replace early spring crops with heat-loving crops such as tomatoes.

To incorporate interplanting creatively into your design, it's helpful to make two lists; one of short-season crops and one of long-season crops. Then add a few notes about each plant's growth habit. For instance, indicate whether it's a cool- or warm-season crop; the space needed to grow the plant; its color, texture, and height; and how many days it takes to mature (this information will be on the seed packet or in the seed catalog). Using this information, pull together combinations from the two lists, combining plants that will be visually pleasing in the design and whose maturity dates work out logistically. You can increase the harvest even more if you use interplanting in conjunction with succession planting.

Succession planting—Succession planting can keep your garden producing from early spring to late fall. It's the method of growing one crop to maturity and then replacing it with another. This is done in one of three ways:

1. Plant a fast-growing, cool-season spring crop, such as radishes or spinach, and replace it with a slower-growing, warm-season crop, such as peppers or tomatoes.

2. Plant a slower-growing, cool-season spring crop, such as broccoli or cabbage, followed by a faster-growing tender crop, such as zucchini or bush beans (tender crops are susceptible to frost damage).

3. Grow a succession of fast-growing crops and match their hardiness to their planting times. For example,

Slower-growing, cool-season spring crops include broccoli and cabbage.

Early in the season, leafy green spinach is ready for harvest, leaving space and time for a succession of one or two more crops.

start with spinach in early spring followed by lettuce. Then plant carrots to round out your fall harvest.

Like interplanting, the trick to successful succession planting is to create combinations that are both visually pleasing and logistically feasible. To make a successive-crop schedule, you will need a calendar, your seed packets (and/or seed catalogs), and a pencil and paper for taking notes. You'll also need to know the average date of your region's last spring frost and first fall frost (again, this information is available

through your county's Cooperative Extension Agent).

To organize your schedule, you will first need to do some simple calculations. Check your seed packets or catalogs to find out the number of days each plant needs to mature. The days to maturity are calculated either from direct seeding to harvest or from transplant to harvest. The majority of maturity dates are calculated from direct seeding to harvest. Those calculated from transplant to harvest are usually tender annuals such as

Sample Successive-Crop Schedule

APRIL	MAY	JUNE	JULY	AUGUST	SEPTEMBER	OCTOBER

Example 1

Start seeds April 23	Transplant to garden May 10	Start harvest June 7	End harvest June 14	*Spinach*		
	Start seeds May 28	Transplant to garden June 14	Start harvest July 13 / End harvest July 27	*Lettuce*		
		Start seeds June 30	Transplant to garden July 27		Start harvest Sept. 22 / End harvest with first frost	*Endive*

Example 2

Start seeds April 15	Transplant to garden May 6	Start harvest June 9	End harvest June 16	*Kohlrabi*		
	Start seeds April 28	Transplant to garden June 16		Start harvest Aug. 23	End harvest with first frost	*Eggplant*

Our last frost date is May 10.

melons, tomatoes, peppers, and eggplants. To establish planting times for these plants, add seven weeks to the number of days the plant takes to mature from a transplant.

For example, your catalog might say 'Purple Beauty' bell peppers take about 70 days to mature from transplant. Add to this number 50 days (7 weeks) to grow the seedling, and you've established that it takes about 120 days to grow a 'Purple Beauty' from seed to first harvest. Now add approximately 14 to 21 days (2 to 3 weeks) for harvesting.

Next, determine the number of days between your region's average last spring frost and first fall frost. If a region's last spring frost occurs on

May 1 and the first fall frost occurs on Oct. 1, this region usually has 153 consecutive frost-free growing days.

Use these calculations to determine how many successions of crops you can grow in each bed. A sample successive-crop schedule is shown above.

For aesthetic purposes, we chose the successions in the example for their similar traits. A garden design requiring a bed of low-growing leafy greens might do well with the succession of spinach, lettuce, and endive. A bed with a purple theme could use the succession of purple kohlrabi followed by eggplant with its purple flowers and fruit. (For tips on starting seedlings for succession planting, see the sidebar on p. 106.)

Starting Seedlings for Succession Planting

If you have planned a successive-crop schedule, you'll be replacing early-spring and summer crops with midseason and fall varieties. That means you will need to start the latter seedlings during the summer. With only a few changes in the procedure, summer seedlings are started in much the same manner as spring seedlings are. The main difference is temperature: Spring crops must deal with cold snaps while summer plantings must contend with heat.

Start your seeds in containers, either indoors or outdoors. If you plant them indoors, south-facing windows may be too hot during summer. Choose east-facing windows or move your containers back from the strong, direct sunlight (fluorescent lights are also a good option). If you sow the seeds outdoors, choose a bright area out of direct sunlight. Late-season, cold-hardy crops such as broccoli, lettuce, and kohlrabi grow best in cool conditions. Start these seedlings outdoors in the shade, under lights in a cool basement, or in a garage.

Once your seeds germinate, transplant them to individual pots or cell flats and move them to a cool, bright outdoor area where there is no chance of them being scorched by the sun. In the same way you acclimated your spring seedlings to cool temperatures, acclimate your summer seedlings to direct sun by gradually exposing them to brighter conditions over several days. Pay close attention to your watering because small containers and cell flats dry out quickly in warm weather.

When it's time to transplant the seedlings into the garden, prepare the beds by completely removing the previous crops and digging additional compost or well-rotted manure into the soil. Then rake the beds smooth. Do your transplanting on a cool evening to let the seedlings settle in overnight.

Remember to water them in thoroughly. If your weather is particularly hot and sunny, protect the transplants with wooden-lath shade covers or construct a temporary shelter by placing tarps, shade cloth, or boards across sawhorses. Over the course of several days, gradually expose the plants to longer periods of direct sunshine. Water regularly and keep the soil cool and moist by applying another good layer of organic mulch.

Starting seeds in flats

In Chapter 3 we showed you how to determine the number of plants you would need to fill your garden. This number will also help you decide the best area in your house to start your seeds. The small number of plants it takes to fill a window box could easily be started on a windowsill. However, a medium-size garden containing roughly 550 plants (approximately 8 flats) may need an area set up in a basement, garage, or spare bedroom.

Choose an area with plenty of warmth and light. Needless to say, the best place to start seeds is in a heated backyard greenhouse. A good second choice is a warm, bright bedroom or windowsill, but with a few adjustments, an insulated garage or basement (that remains well above freezing) is just as suitable. If you supply bottom heat with electric cables or mats and artificial light with either fluorescent tubes or grow lamps, your seeds should sprout and flourish in these otherwise dark rooms. (For a list of materials needed to start seeds, see the sidebar on p. 108.)

Sterilizing flats

Hygiene is one of the most important factors in successful plant propagation. Pots and flats that have been used in previous years should be sterilized in a 10% bleach solution and then rinsed with clean water. If we have a lot of containers and tools that need disinfecting, we fill our deep laundry sink with the solution, which allows plenty of room to dip flats and makes rinsing them easy.

Nonsterilized equipment and soil can lead to damping-off, which is a disease caused by water and soil-borne fungi. Damping-off spreads quickly, withering the stems and roots of young seedlings. If your seedlings topple over at the soil line, throw them out, and don't reuse the infected soil mix. Other ways to combat damping-off are to sow seeds thinly, to keep the growing area well ventilated, and to apply the correct amount of water—don't overwater.

Seeding into flats

After proper sterilization, you can begin seeding. Fill your clean containers or flats with planting medium.

Scatter small seeds such as lettuce into open flats. Once they germinate, transplant them to cell flats where they will grow until planting time.

Materials List for Starting Seeds

Flats and containers

FLATS AND CONTAINERS

From paper cups and egg cartons to actual nursery pots and plug flats, any variety of containers can be used to start seeds as long as they have adequate drainage holes.

After trying a variety of containers over the years, we found that standard 11-in. by 21-in. open flats (flats without individual cells) and flats containing 72 square cells best suited our needs. We start the majority of our seeds in the open flats and then transplant to the cell flats. Most of the seedlings grow in cell flats until planting time without additional potting up (planting into a succession of larger pots). However, several varieties need extra room to grow, such as squash, sunflowers, and cucumbers, which we start in 2-in. to 4-in. pots. We start tender crops, such as eggplants, peppers, and tomatoes, in cell flats and transplant them to larger pots until we plant them outside well after the danger of frost has passed.

GROWING MEDIUM

Good planting medium for seed starting should be sterile, free of weed seeds and insects, fine in texture, and moisture retentive. Although it is possible to make your own, it's easier to buy com-

COLD FRAMES

Whether you construct a permanent cold frame from wood and glass or a quick, temporary cloche made with wire hoops and plastic, a protective shelter for seedlings is one of the most useful tools for a gardener (for more on cold frames, see p. 111).

FERTILIZERS

Once young seedlings become established in their pots or flats and are growing well in the cold frame, nourish them with an all-purpose liquid fertilizer. Young seedlings burn easily, so dilute the solution to half the normal recommended strength.

Growing medium

SEEDS

Many seeds remain viable for years, but for optimum germination, buy fresh seeds each year. Read your seed packets carefully for special growing instructions. Also, store seeds in a dry, cool, well-ventilated place.

WATERING IMPLEMENTS

Watering newly seeded flats must be done carefully. A large gush of water can quickly dislodge tiny seeds, sweeping them all to one side of the container or burying them under too much soil. Use a watering can with a fine rose (or tip). If you are starting your seeds in a greenhouse or garage where a hose can be used, a "fog" nozzle is ideal for delivering a fine mist to minute seeds and seedlings.

mercial potting soil or soilless mix. These blends are made from various combinations of peat moss, vermiculite, perlite, sand, and nutrients. Check the label to make sure it is formulated for starting seeds.

GROW LIGHTS

Your seedlings will require about 16 hours of light per day. Even if your indoor growing area is beside a bright, south-facing window, you may need to supplement the natural light with either fluorescent lights or grow lamps (if you use a fluorescent shop-light fixture, equip it with one cool and one warm fluorescent tube for the broadest spectrum of light). For best results, hang the lights approximately 6 in. to 8 in. above the foliage.

LABELS

Each flat or container will need a label. Avoid using the paper seed packets as labels because they quickly biodegrade before the season is over. We use sturdy white plastic or wooden labels and write out the information in pencil (many felt-tipped markers are not permanent and wash off or fade in the sun). When we transplant the seedlings into the garden, their markers go with them. Durable labels can be reused over several seasons if they are sterilized each year and brought in for the winter months.

PROPAGATION
HEATING CABLES
OR MATS *(optional)*

Most seeds germinate quickly in soil temperatures of 68°F to 86°F. Electric propagation heating cables or mats provide gentle, bottom heat (follow the manufacturer's recommendations for setting up a growing area with these devices). Flats placed above heating cables or mats need to be checked carefully. The soil surface may be moist, but at the bottom of the flat, near the heat source, the soil can become bone dry.

Fog nozzle and watering can

A cold frame does not need to be fancy to grow vigorous seedlings.

Settle the soil by lightly rapping the container on a tabletop. Fill in any low spots with additional medium. The soil mix should be almost level with the rim of the flat so that air can easily circulate around the seedlings. Thoroughly dampen the soil with warm water and set the flats aside to drain.

Seeds are sown in containers and flats in a variety of ways. Sow large seeds, such as spinach, by dropping them one by one into the individual tray cells. Gently firm each seed into the soil and then cover it with a light sprinkling of soil mix. With no additional potting up, these seeds will germinate and grow in the same flat until planting time. Small seeds, such as lettuce, are difficult to sow individually into cells, so you have to scatter

them evenly onto the soil surface in open flats or pots. Cover them with a sprinkling of soil mix unless the seed packet indicates they need light to germinate. If they do need light, do not cover them with additional growing medium. Water the flats with warm water and keep them evenly moist—but not soggy—at all times.

In most cases, flower and vegetable seeds will germinate at room temperature. However, the process can be accelerated by keeping the soil temperature between 68°F and 86°F (check individual seed packets for best germination temperatures). You can increase the soil temperature by placing the seeded flats near a heater or woodstove or by placing them above electric propagation heating cables or mats.

Once the seeds germinate, they no longer need bottom heat. At this point, seedlings can become leggy if the air temperature indoors is too warm and there is not adequate light. To prevent this, place flats near south-facing windows or provide extra illumination with either fluorescent lights or grow lights.

When the seeds that were scattered into open flats are large enough to handle by their leaves, carefully "thin out" (transplant) the seedlings. A pencil is helpful for this process. Simply lift each small plant out of the loose soil mix with the pencil point, keeping the roots intact. Always handle seedlings by their leaves, never by their fragile stems. Transplant the tiny seedlings to cell flats. With your finger or pencil point, make a hole in the moist planting medium of each cell. Carefully lower the roots of the seedling into the hole. Firm the soil around the roots and stem and finish with a light watering of warm water. It is important to thin out the seedlings as soon as possible so they don't become overcrowded and intertwined. Return your newly transplanted flats to their bright location.

Once the tiny seedlings have established themselves for a week or so indoors, begin acclimating them to the cooler, brighter conditions of a cold frame over several days. Place the flats in a cold frame during the day for increasingly longer periods of time and bring them in at night. After a few days—weather permitting— leave them in the cold frame full time (continue to bring tender annuals, such as melons, tomatoes, eggplants, and peppers, indoors at night until nighttime temperatures moderate to around 45°F). If daytime temperatures in your region are too cold to move tiny seedlings out so soon, keep them growing indoors near bright windows (supplemented with fluorescent or grow lights if necessary) until it warms up outside.

From flats to cold frames

Cold frames can be used throughout the year for various plant protection and propagation needs, but they are invaluable in early spring for starting young seedlings. If you are growing a small garden, your cold frame could be a simple tunnel cloche constructed from a sheet of plastic secured to a series of wire

These healthy seedlings show good root development.

Phlox

Ageratum

Starting Seedlings for Border Plants

The border plants in your design add color and define the pattern. Use low-growing, compact varieties with colorful flowers or foliage, such as parsley, dusty miller, marigolds, pansies, alyssum, lobelia, phlox, and ageratum. You can easily start large numbers of these plants using the following techniques.

For parsley, marigolds, pansies, phlox, ageratum, and dusty miller, use the planting techniques for starting small seeds described on p. 110. Parsley is slow to germinate, so be patient. Ageratum and dusty miller need light to germinate, so don't cover them with additional soil mix. Pansies need to be chilled for two or three days prior to being planted to break their dormancy. Place a damp paper towel on a saucer, sprinkle the seeds onto the surface, and put the saucer in the refrigerator (keeping the towel damp at all times). Once they are done

Alyssum

Marigolds

Lobelia

Pansies

chilling, scatter the pansy seeds onto growing medium in an open flat and lightly cover them with additional soil mix. Once the seeds have germinated, thin out the individual seedlings and transplant them to cell flats.

Alyssum seeds are easy to start. Simply fill cell flats with growing medium and evenly scatter the seeds across the surface so that approximately three to five seeds cover each square inch. Alyssum seeds need light to germinate, so no soil covering is needed. They will germinate and grow in the same flat until planting time.

Lobelia seeds are started in exactly the same way. However, they are so minute that it may be difficult to scatter them thinly and evenly. If you discover overcrowding when the seeds germinate, simply thin out small clumps of seedlings and transplant them to new cell flats. Both lobelia and alyssum are especially susceptible to damping-off, and despite your best preventative measures, a light application of fungicide may be necessary. Some people have success using chamomile tea as an organic, fungicidal spray.

Parsley

Dusty miller

Potting up is necessary when you see more roots than soil. These root-bound seedlings are ready to be moved into larger containers.

ture inside a closed cold frame can soar. When mild weather is forecast, leave the frame open a generous crack before going to work in the morning and close it as soon as you get home to preserve as much heat as possible for the night.

If nighttime temperatures dip to near freezing, there are several ways to protect seedlings. If you are growing only a few flats, it's best to bring them indoors. However, this is impractical if you are growing many flats. Instead, provide insulation over your cold frame by covering it with old blankets, burlap, or carpeting (very unattractive yet very effective). Remove the covering in the morning to let in the light and warmth. Along with an insulating cover, the air temperature inside your frame can be elevated a few degrees with light bulbs or heating cables. We hang two chicken brooder lamps equipped with regular 100-watt bulbs in each of our 6-ft. by 8-ft. cold frames (the lights are 2 ft. above the foliage).

Caring for seedlings

Cold frames provide bright light, warm daytime temperatures, and cool nighttime temperatures: perfect conditions for growing plants. With a little extra nurturing and protection from you, your seedlings will mature into vigorous transplants in a matter of weeks.

Monitor the soil moisture in your flats twice a day. Flat cells dry out quickly in warm weather. Use a watering can when seedlings are small and graduate to the efficiency of a hose-end sprayer as they grow. If possible, water in the morning so the seedlings have a chance to dry off during the day, reducing the risk

hoops. This style of cloche is inexpensive and easy to make, but it is only temporary and can take a beating in windy weather. If you plan to grow a medium-size or large garden year after year, it would be wise to build a permanent cold frame.

Place a covering on the ground before you construct your cold frame or cloche to reduce slug, weed, and insect problems. A piece of porous landscape fabric is suitable in a temporary cloche, while landscape fabric covered with a layer of gravel works well in a permanent cold frame. Avoid using plastic as a ground covering because water will collect on top and may rot the seedlings.

Monitor your cold frame at least twice a day. Even in cool weather, if the sun is shining, the air tempera-

of disease. Frequent watering will eventually leach nutrients from potting soil. So when seedlings are a couple of weeks old, begin fertilizing them with an all-purpose liquid fertilizer reduced by half the recommended strength.

As we previously mentioned, it's important to open the cold frame a generous crack to regulate air temperature. This also promotes air circulation, which is vital in a warm, humid cold frame where damping-off might occur.

Various pests can also present problems in a cold frame. For instance, the warm, cozy conditions you provide your seedlings are very appealing to mice. These little critters can do substantial damage as they rummage through the flats looking for stray seeds. Two weeks before we put our flats out, we set mouse traps in the empty cold frames and then continue trapping throughout the early spring. Slugs can creep in and mow down an amazing number of seedlings in one night. Handpicking the pests is your best defense. If you notice damaged seedlings in the morning, check under the nearby flats until you find the offenders (slugs usually hide in the deep crevices on the underside of cell flats). We rarely have insect problems because the weather is cool in early spring and the frames are closed much of the time.

As the seedlings grow, choose mild days to open the cold frame completely to let the seedlings "breathe" and be jostled by the wind. The cool air will keep the young seedlings stocky, and the movement from the breeze will produce strong stems. Just remember to close the frame at night.

If bad weather delays your projected planting date or certain plants grow faster than expected, some seedlings may become root bound. To determine if any seedlings are root bound, carefully lift a sampling out of the trays and inspect their roots. If you see more roots than soil, you will need to transplant the seedlings to slightly larger pots or tray cells (called potting up). The newly transplanted seedlings can continue to grow in the cold frame unhindered until planting time. Use this method to determine when slow-growing, tender annuals,

A nursery with signs explaining plant care and characteristics will help you make informed decisions for your garden design.

such as tomatoes, eggplants, and peppers, need to be transplanted to larger pots.

Hardening off seedlings

Hardening off seedlings is the process of gradually acclimating them to harsher outdoor conditions. This procedure started when you moved the small sprouts from your house to your cold frame. Even switching from the gentle sprinkles of a watering can to the shower of a hose-end sprayer helps toughen your seedlings. As the weeks pass and temperatures warm, it's time to finish the process so that your young plants are no longer dependent on the cold frame for protection.

About 10 days before you transplant your seedlings into the garden, leave the cold frame open for increasingly longer periods until it is open full time. As always, watch your outdoor thermometer and close the frame if temperatures are near freezing. Continue to bring tomatoes, eggplants, and peppers in at night until nighttime temperatures are above 45°F.

BUYING SEEDLINGS

Starting flowers and vegetables from seed requires a commitment of time and space. If you are short on either, consider buying seedlings from a local nursery for transplanting.

Locate a reputable greenhouse or garden center that sells healthy, well-cared-for plants. Young seedlings should be stocky, with sturdy stems and bright-green foliage. Always avoid wilted, root-bound, leggy, or insect-infested plants. Seedlings stressed by improper care may not develop properly or, worse, may not survive after transplanting.

Filling a medium-size or large garden with nursery-grown seedlings can be expensive. If the cost is prohibitive, consider a combination of homegrown and purchased seedlings. Certain varieties or large quantities of any one plant may not be available at your local nursery. So plan to start these plants at home. For example, your local garden center may not carry 145 parsley plants at any one time. Starting this many parsley seedlings at home does not require a lot of time or space because they are easy to germinate and only occupy two flats.

Finally, take note of where your seedlings were grown. If they were in a greenhouse or sheltered area, they will need to be hardened off before you plant them in your garden. You don't necessarily need a cold frame for this process. Instead, place the flats close to your house. If nighttime temperatures drop to near freezing, loosely cover the flats with a blanket and remove it in the morning. Over the course of several days, move the flats farther away from the protection of the house wall. When nighttime temperatures remain well above freezing, you can leave the covering off.

*Buy your seedlings from a reputable,
well-maintained nursery.*

*Watch your graph-paper plan come to life
as you plant your new kitchen garden.*

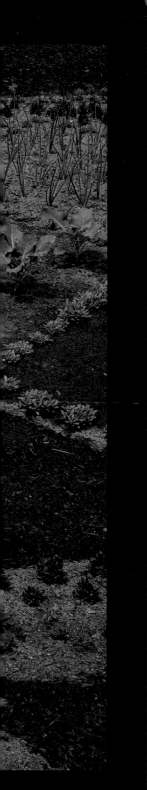

chapter five

From Graph Paper to Garden

*W*hen the long winter months are over and spring finally arrives, a gardener's work pace quickens. After months of planning and anticipation, turning your graph-paper plan into a beautiful kitchen garden is about to become a reality. But first, the garden soil needs to be prepared and fertilized, your design must be laid out on the freshly tilled soil, and the garden features—such as structures, paths, and, most important, the plants—need to be installed. To keep your new kitchen garden growing vigorously, you will also need to maintain your garden routinely, but your hard work will be generously rewarded at harvest time.

GARDEN PREPARATION

Once you have finished your garden design and have chosen the appropriate plant varieties, it's time to get your hands dirty. Transferring your design from the graph-paper plan to your garden is quite simple. However, take your time. Measure accurately and prepare the soil thoroughly. A little extra effort spent at this stage in the process will help ensure a beautiful design and a garden full of healthy plants.

Measuring and squaring up the perimeter

Begin your new kitchen garden by defining its boundaries on your chosen site. You will need your graph-paper plan (see Chapter 2), a measuring tape, stakes, string, and an assistant.

If the garden is square, use your graph-paper plan as a guide to measure the perimeter and place a stake at each of the four corners. Before driving the stakes into the earth, make sure the corners are square by measuring diagonally from corner to corner. Keep moving the stakes until the diagonal measurements are equal. The corners are now square and you can pound the stakes in place and define the perimeter with string. Making sure the perimeter lines are square is particularly important because all the interior lines will be measured from them.

To determine the perimeter for a circular garden design, start by pounding a short length of pipe into the center of your garden site (conduit or PVC pipe works well). Loosely tie a string around the pipe. Measure out half the diameter of your desired circle and tie a sharpened stake at this point on the string. To make a perfect circle, use the stake and string like a large compass. Keep the string taut and walk in a circle around the center pipe, leaving a line scored in the ground.

Removing sod

If your new kitchen garden will be located on an area of lawn, the sod will need to be removed. This can be done by cutting and removing individual squares of sod or by tilling the lawn under. We don't recommend the use of herbicides in areas intended for vegetable production.

Cutting and removing sod by hand is hard work, but in the end you are left with a beautiful, grass-free area ready for fertilizing and tilling. You will need a sharp edging shovel or a square-bladed spade. Just as you would cut a large sheet cake, slice the sod into a grid pattern and cut evenly around the perimeter, using the string as a guide. Sod is very heavy, so keep the squares small. Use the spade to cut under each square of sod, leaving as much soil as possible in the garden area. You can use these pieces of sod to fill in bare spots on your lawn, or you can compost them (sod containing tenacious perennial weeds, such as quack grass, is not recommended for compost piles because the weeds may not die).

If you are planning a large garden and think cutting and removing the sod by hand would be too time-consuming and backbreaking, consider tilling the grass under. Trying to penetrate dense sod with a front-tine tiller is exhausting, so we suggest using a rear-tine tiller.

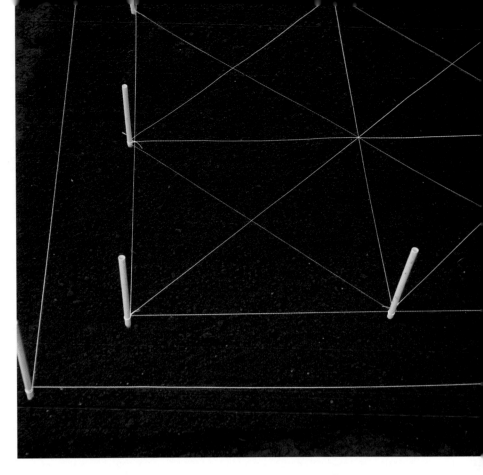

Begin tilling the area during the summer or fall before you plan to plant. Run the tiller over the area several times until the clumps of sod are shredded into fine bits. Gather up any large remaining pieces by hand and throw them in the compost pile. Let the soil rest for several days, allowing weeds and grasses to sprout up again, and then immediately till them under. The shredded grass and weeds will compost in the soil. In the fall, plant a cover crop such as hairy vetch or white Dutch clover to protect the bare ground from erosion and to prevent nutrients from leaching through the soil during the winter. In the spring, till the cover crop under, which will add extra organic matter to the soil.

Amending the soil

To create a lush kitchen garden, fertilizers may be required to maintain proper plant growth and vegetable production. Garden centers carry large displays of fertilizers, both chemical and natural. Chemical fertilizers give an instant boost of nutrients to the plants, but they require repeated applications and do nothing to enhance the soil structure.

Whether your garden is large or small, plant growth will be enhanced by adding organic matter to the soil. We amend our soil with equal amounts of peat moss, compost, and aged, well-rotted manure and then work these amendments into the soil by hand or by tilling. Amending the soil with these natural materials provides nutrients, lightens the soil, and increases the soil's ability to retain moisture. Do not use fresh manure because it is "hot" (containing high levels of ammonia) and can damage seedlings and young plants. If you

For a crisp design, accurately measure the placement of stakes using your graph-paper plan as a guide.

have fresh manure, work it into the soil in the fall to allow it time to "mellow" over the winter months. You can apply well-rotted manure in the spring without adversely affecting seedlings.

Organic amendments improve soil texture and provide a good nutrient base simultaneously. However, vegetable plants are heavy feeders and may require additional natural fertilizers. This is especially true if you are creating a new garden on soil that has not been previously cultivated and amended.

The three major plant foods are nitrogen, phosphorus, and potassium. Along with magnesium, sulfur, calcium, and small amounts of trace elements, they all contribute to healthy plant growth in many ways. Nitrogen, for example, promotes healthy leaf and stem growth. Crops

Double Digging

If you are creating a new garden on compacted soil or want to amend individual beds within a garden, double digging will improve drainage and work the amendments deep into the root zone. Although this process is labor intensive, it should only need to be done once. If the beds are not walked on, simply amending and turning the soil will be sufficient in subsequent years.

Once you have the design staked out, add approximately equal amounts of compost, peat moss, and well-rotted manure to the bed. These amendments provide nutrients, lighten the soil, and increase the soil's ability to retain moisture. Depending on the needs of your soil, you can incorporate organic fertilizers, lime, or sulfur at this time. Liberally broadcast the amendments on

Broadcast equal amounts of the soil amendments to a depth of 2 in. to 4 in.

Dig a trench one spade deep along one side of the bed, placing the topsoil in a wheelbarrow. Use a spading fork to loosen the subsoil in the bottom of the trench.

such as spinach, Swiss chard, and cabbage all relish nitrogen-rich soil. Blood meal is a terrific concentrated source of nitrogen. But use it sparingly to prevent burning tender young plants.

Flower and fruit development are enhanced with the presence of phosphorus. Tomato, cucumber, and

squash will all benefit from an application of phosphorus in the form of bonemeal or rock phosphate. Bonemeal is lightly broadcast over the surface of the soil and turned under. Rock phosphate needs to be cultivated deep into the root zone where it will remain and slowly release for up to five years.

the soil surface to a depth of 2 in. to 4 in. (see the left photo on the facing page).

After spreading the amendments, dig a trench one spade deep along one side of the bed. Remove the topsoil and place it in a wheelbarrow. With a spading fork, loosen the subsoil in the bottom of the trench (see the right photo on the facing page). If your soil is particularly poor, more compost and rotted manure can be worked into this lower layer.

Dig another trench one spade deep, adjacent to the first, and place this soil in the first trench (see the left photo below). Again, loosen the subsoil with a spading fork. As you work, break up the large chunks until the soil is light and crumbly. Work backwards so the freshly cultivated soil is never walked on and compressed. Repeat this process across the entire bed.

Fill the final trench with the soil you removed from the first trench (see the right photo below) and then rake the entire bed smooth. The lofty, rich soil in the bed will be several inches higher than the surrounding paths—perfect conditions for growing robust vegetables.

Dig another trench one spade deep, adjacent to the first, and place soil from this trench in the first. Again, loosen the subsoil with a spading fork.

Fill the final trench with the soil you removed from the first trench and then rake the bed smooth.

Potassium encourages vigorous root development. Root crops, such as onions and beets, will grow well in soil amended with potassium-rich kelp meal, greensand, or wood ashes.

Fertilizing doesn't need to be complicated. Complete organic fertilizers containing appropriate amounts of nitrogen (N), phosphorous (P), potassium (K), and other nutrients can be found at most garden centers. The amount of the three major plant foods (N-P-K) will be listed in the same order on the fertilizer label. Amending your soil in the spring with an application of a complete organic fertilizer and humus will most likely be all the nutrients your garden

Amending the soil with approximately equal amounts of compost, peat moss, and well-rotted manure provides nutrients, lightens the soil, and increases the soil's ability to retain moisture.

will need for the growing season. If the occasional plant looks a bit peaked during the summer, give it a boost with a solution of fish emulsion, manure tea, or a side dressing of an organic fertilizer.

In addition to fertilizing, you should perform a simple soil test to determine the pH level of your soil. A pH test, measured on a scale of 0 to 14, will reveal the level of your soil's acidity or alkalinity (0 to 6.9 is acid, 7 is neutral, and 7.1 to 14 is alkaline). For most flowers and vegetables, you need to maintain a pH of about 6.5 to 6.8. If your pH level is too low (acid soil), add lime. If your pH level is too high (alkaline soil), add sulfur. Start by adding small amounts of either lime or sulfur and retest the soil until it is at an optimum pH level.

Tilling

It's not practical to till a small garden because it is easily turned over and raked smooth by hand. However, if you are creating a medium-size to large garden, tilling becomes very practical.

You can till and amend the soil in a medium-size garden in one fast and easy step. Simply broadcast a 2-in. to 4-in. layer of peat moss, compost, well-rotted manure, and any other necessary fertilizers over the entire garden and till it in to a depth of about 8 in. You are now ready to stake out your design.

Unfortunately, this is not a good method to use in a large garden. A large garden has paths within it, and the valuable amendments would be wasted in the paths. It's better to till the entire garden area to eradicate weeds and to provide a smooth surface. Then stake out the design and amend the individual beds by hand using the double-digging method (see the sidebar on p. 122).

Measuring and staking out the design

If you removed the perimeter strings to allow access with a tiller, you will need to reposition them so that you can begin staking out the interior design, or pattern. For this job, bring along your graph-paper plan, a measuring tape, stakes, and string. Staking out the design is easier if you have an assistant.

Using the dots on your graph-paper plan as a guide, measure out the placement of each stake. Start at the perimeter and work inward, measuring and positioning the stakes as you go. Try to walk only on the areas that will eventually be the paths so you don't compact the freshly tilled soil in the bed areas. When all the stakes have been placed, run string to delineate the pattern. It's helpful to use two colors of string when laying out a knot-garden design (see the Celtic knot garden on p. 63).

INSTALLATION OF GARDEN FEATURES

Once the beds are prepared and the garden design is well defined with string, it's time to install the garden features. With each component you add, your garden will slowly begin to take shape. Install the structures and paths first and finish with the plants and mulch.

Adding structures

Structures set the mood of your garden, add height, and become part of the permanent framework that provides interest during the winter months. These items are installed first in the garden and might include trellises, fences, arbors, and permanent edgings.

After amending and double digging the beds in our large kitchen garden, we cut to size flexible 4-in. cedar bender boards (which are thin strips of cedar available at most home and garden centers) and use them to edge each bed. This kept the path materials from migrating into the beds and vice versa. Next, we tackled the big job of installing the fencing and the connecting arbor. These were wonderful additions to the garden, offering vertical growing space and a barrier to animals. (For ease in construction, very large features, such as gazebos, garden sheds,

A variety of materials can be used for paths: back row (from left to right)—compost, straw, peat moss; middle row—grass clippings, ground bark, sawdust; front row—bricks, gravel, and sod.

and fountains, are best installed before the beds have been laid out.)

This is also a good time to position temporary features that will reside in the center of the beds. These items might include statues, potted plants, bean-pole tripods, or a birdbath. It is easier to install these features now, rather than after the plants are in position.

Adding paths

Permanent paths are installed next in your garden. Whether your design calls for gravel, stone, brick, sod, or cement pavers, you'll want your paths to look attractive and provide years of service. Take the time to install them correctly. For example, if you are laying in a gravel path, first level the ground and put down landscape fabric to discourage weeds. Paths of brick or paving stones require a well-prepared foundation of crushed stone and sand (there are many garden reference books that give complete installation instructions). Your extra effort now will result in a permanent walkway you can enjoy for years.

If you've decided to make an annual garden that can be totally turned under, choose a path material that is biodegradable, such as sawdust, peat moss, nut hulls, or bark chips. For a less-formal look, use straw, hay, or grass clippings. Biodegradable path materials can be applied either before or after the plants are in place. Install your chosen path material using the string lines and stakes as a guide. This will ensure straight paths and crisp corners.

Planting

Once the days become warmer and the nighttime temperatures no longer dip below freezing, it's finally planting time. Either your careful scheduling has produced a cold frame full of tiny seedlings or the back of your car is loaded with flats from a local nursery. In either case, the anticipation of planting a new garden design is always exciting.

The process is very simple. Choose a mild day, preferably with overcast skies, so the plants are not stressed by the hot sun. Assemble your freshly watered flats near the prepared garden beds and have your graph-paper plan close at hand.

Make a final check of the specific spacing requirements of each plant variety before you begin. One by one, pop the seedlings out of their trays, being careful to preserve as much soil as possible around the roots. Referring to your graph-paper plan, plant the seedlings along the string guidelines. Plants such as lettuce, lobelia, and alyssum prefer to be planted at the same depth they were in their containers. For support, plant long-stemmed varieties such as cabbage, broccoli, and tomatoes farther down so that the soil line is even with their first set of leaves. With all plants, firm the soil around their roots and thoroughly water them in.

The tiny seedlings do their best to make the design visible. However, it will take several more weeks for the plants to develop and begin to fill in the beds.

Mulching

Newly planted seedlings nestled into rich, brown, freshly tilled soil always look wonderful. But before long, the soil will become a carpet of tiny, green weed sprouts. Applying a 2-in. to 4-in. layer of organic mulch before weeds germinate should suppress most weeds, saving you hours of weeding. If occasional renegades pop up, you can easily pluck them from the fluffy layer of mulch. During the summer, mulches reduce moisture evaporation by shielding the soil from the drying effects of the wind and sun. In the fall they can be turned under, adding valuable humus to the soil.

Organic mulches include grass clippings, straw, sawdust, peat moss, compost, various nut hulls, and chopped leaves. Each has its own color and texture, which can be used to coordinate with the mood of your garden. For instance, we used peat moss because its brown color provided a dark background to show off the vibrant plants. It also presented a formal appearance. Straw, on the other hand, can lighten a dark color scheme, while its rough texture conveys a casual feeling.

Keep in mind a few precautions when using certain mulches. Grass clippings should be scattered in a thin layer no more than 2 in. thick. Any thicker, and the layer will form a mat that reduces air circulation to the soil below. Keep peat moss and compost slightly pulled back from plant stems; otherwise, their moisture-retaining qualities may cause fungus and rot. Sawdust and some nut hulls can be slow to decompose and may temporarily rob nitrogen from the soil when turned under. If necessary, in the spring apply a nitrogen-rich organic fertilizer such as blood meal. Grain kernels left behind by the harvester can sprout in straw mulch, but you can easily pull them out or smother them by adding another layer of mulch. These minor drawbacks are far outweighed by the benefits mulching provides.

Mulching is the final step in constructing your new kitchen garden. Once you have finished spreading the mulch, remove the stakes and strings from the garden area.

GARDEN MAINTENANCE

Congratulations! Much of the hard work is behind you. You've installed your garden structures, laid out the paths, put in the plants, and added mulch. However, maintenance of your new garden has just begun. Paying attention to detail as you maintain your garden not only keeps your landscape trim and tidy but also results in higher fruit and vegetable yields. By staying in tune with your garden, you can prevent problems before they start. Take a quick daily walking tour to assess the various needs of your plants: Check the soil's moisture, look for insect pests, and decide what plants will soon need trimming and staking. As you stroll, pluck out a few weeds and deadhead a flower or two. This way there will be less to do on the weekend.

Dealing with spring frosts

At this point in your garden preparations, you've come too far to let an unexpected late spring frost ruin all your hard work. Spring weather can be very fickle. Even if you carefully scheduled your planting time to occur after your region's last projected frost date, a warm, sunny day can unexpectedly turn into a crisp, frosty night.

Once young seedlings have been planted, keep a close watch on the temperature gauge and weather reports. If nighttime temperatures will dip to near freezing, protect tender plants, such as melons, tomatoes, eggplants, and peppers. You can use an overturned flower pot to create an instant cloche for a single plant or construct a protective tunnel cloche from wire hoops and plastic for a group of plants. Another option is to drape entire beds with two or three layers of a floating row cover (a lightweight, mesh fabric normally used for bug protection) or a sheet of plastic. Condensation on plastic can freeze and damage tender young leaves if they touch. So if you use plastic, secure it to short stakes so the material "hovers" above the plants.

Controlling diseases and pests

Once you are past the danger of frost, your next concern will be controlling diseases and pests. Take heart in the fact that a well-maintained garden is less likely to foster diseases and that healthy plants will have increased tolerance to pests. However, for those that do invade, there are many organic solutions to prevent or reduce damage.

Where plant diseases (viruses, bacteria, and fungi) are concerned, it's best to prevent problems before they start. Prevention begins in the winter with your seed order. Choose varieties that have been developed to resist certain diseases. For instance, some tomatoes are resistant to verticillium or fusarium wilt (refer to your seed catalogs for specific disease-resistant varieties). Lessen the damp, cluttered conditions that encourage plant disease by watering in the early morning and by keeping your garden clear of debris. It's also important to keep a yearly crop rotation schedule and to do a thorough fall cleanup, burning any infected plants.

Water in the early morning before the onset of a hot summer day to minimize moisture evaporation.

While prevention is the best method for dealing with disease, you may need several defensive measures to combat insects. Barriers, traps, beneficial organisms, and sprays can all be put to use. It's best to start with the least-invasive methods and increase your defenses as necessary.

Begin by closely monitoring your plants on your daily garden stroll. Many insects, larvae, and slugs can be handpicked from the plants. In the case of aphids, a good spray of water from a hose is usually all that is needed to dislodge and kill the tiny green bugs.

Setting up barriers around and over your plants before the insects discover your newly planted garden is very effective. For instance, you can usually keep cutworms at bay by encircling young seedlings with 3-in.-high bands of heavy paper or lightweight cardboard (push 1 in. into the soil and leave 2 in. above ground). To prevent damage from flying insects, drape a floating row cover over your plants. Row covers are lightweight, allowing water and sunlight to pass through easily, and won't hinder plant growth. Secure the cover edges with stones, boards, or small piles of soil so that pests cannot slip under or penetrate any gaps in the material. We realize your garden design is meant to be a focal point and not hidden beneath bug cloth, but in early spring, row covers protect young seedlings from pests and chilly nights. Once the plants are well established, remove the covers (be aware that other pest-prevention measures may need to be implemented once the row cover has been taken away).

Trapping is another effective method of battling insects. You can catch Japanese beetles, whiteflies, and many other pests with commercial sticky traps and scent-alluring traps. You can also make your own. For example, by placing shallow containers of beer in the garden, you'll draw slugs into them, where they will drown. Leaving a board or a piece of black plastic on the ground overnight will provide an attractive hiding place for slugs, snails, and other bugs, allowing you to dispose of them in the morning.

The presence of beneficial animals, insects, and bacteria will also decrease your pest population. Frogs, toads, and birds eat a variety of slugs and insects. Centipedes, spiders, parasitic wasps, and ladybugs also do their share to eradicate garden-ravaging whiteflies, mealybugs, and aphids. One of the most fascinating and useful organic insecticides is *Bacillus thuringiensis* (Bt). This beneficial bacteria can be purchased through catalogs and at garden centers. It is safe for plants, humans, pets, and other vertebrates, yet it is effective against armyworms, hornworms, Colorado potato beetle larvae, imported cabbageworms, and cabbage loopers. When a caterpillar or larvae ingests the bacteria, it permeates their stomach lining, resulting in paralysis and death to the pest. You might also try commercially available insecticidal soaps that effectively eliminate soft-bodied pests, including aphids, mealybugs, and whiteflies.

In the event your bug population turns into an infestation, you may need to resort to potent plant-derived insecticides. Two of the most commonly used are pyrethrum and rotenone. Although they are organic and break down quickly, these powerful pesticides should be used as a last recourse. Carefully follow the instructions on the label and be aware that they kill beneficial insects along with the pests.

Watering

The moisture content of the soil is perhaps the most important factor to evaluate on a daily basis. When and how much to water are determined by the soil, weather, plant variety, the area in which the plant is grown, and the plant's stage of growth.

For example, plants in clay pots, window boxes, and container gardens may need watering every day. The hot summer sun and dry wind can quickly evaporate the water in these small containers. Germinating seeds and young seedlings will also need daily monitoring to prevent them from drying out. Keep them evenly moist at all times but not soggy. Once the seedlings have established themselves, give the soil regular, thorough soakings rather than frequent light waterings. This will encourage their roots to grow deep into the soil, reducing their risk of drying out between soakings. As the plants mature and their fruits and vegetables begin to appear and swell, they must receive adequate water to achieve their delicious, full potential.

There are several ways to conserve precious water. The garden prepara-

Stroll through your garden daily with a basket or bucket in hand for quick spot weeding and deadheading. We use an old berry-picking flat to hold weeds and spent flower blooms.

tion and planning you did in the spring will reduce the amount of water applied to your garden beds during the hot days of July and August. For example, the organic matter you added to your soil along with a top dressing of mulch will substantially increase the water-retaining abilities of your soil and reduce evaporation. Intensively planted beds will also conserve water. As the plants mature, their leaves will touch one another, shading the soil from the drying effects of the sun.

The best time to water is in the morning. If you wait until the afternoon, much of the water will be wasted to evaporation. Evening waterings may not allow the plants time to dry

off before sundown, which might
result in increased fungal infestations
due to prolonged damp conditions.

There are many varieties of watering implements on the market, including watering cans, watering
wands, sprinklers, and soaker hoses.
The size of your garden and your
plants' individual needs will determine the best watering device. In early spring when the plants are small,
we use overhead sprinklers for easy
watering. As the season continues,
we switch to hand watering, which allows us to soak the soil without soak-
ing the foliage and flowers. This
reduces the possibility of fungus and
mildew and keeps the flower borders
standing upright rather than bent
over from the weight of the water.

Weeding

All gardens have weeds. But you can
ease this plight in several ways: by design, mulching, and perseverance.

Controlling weeds starts with your
basic garden design. Be realistic
about how much time you have to
maintain your garden. During the
winter months, as we design and
gather inspiration from garden
books and seed catalogs, our
enthusiasm sometimes gets the
best of us. The lavish gardens we
envision in our minds never have
weeds! It's best to start small. A tidy,
easily maintained area will bring
more joy and relaxation than a large,
overwhelming garden. Each year, expand your small garden as your
schedule allows.

Mulching, as we discussed earlier in this chapter, is one of the best ways to control weeds. However, it's not a cure-all, especially if your new garden site was previously inhabited by weeds. For those weeds that do find their way through the mulch, your best defense is to pull them immediately. Established weeds are time-consuming to eradicate. In addition, they compete for nutrients with your flower and vegetable crops and can quickly shade them out.

Garden centers and catalogs are full of helpful weeding tools, each with its own specialty. For instance, a basic garden hoe is perfect for quickly slicing off a weed coming up through a mulched path. We prefer to weed intensively planted beds by hand. Close spacing between plants leaves little room for a pronged hand cultivator. Its unforgiving tines can quickly damage root crops and young seedlings.

To lessen your weeding time with each passing year, never let a weed go to seed (easier said than done!). Since we know they're here to stay, try to make the best of the situation. Weeding in the cool, early morning air can actually be quite enjoyable.

Trimming and staking plants

Trimming and staking the plants in your kitchen garden is essential to maintaining its beautiful pattern and appearance. Overgrown foliage can quickly blur the design and invite insect and fungal infestations.

The majority of your trimming chores will occur naturally as you harvest. You'll need to watch the flower borders closely, especially some varieties of alyssum and

A well-maintained garden looks tidy and produces healthy, lush vegetables.

To give the young cucumber vines proper air circulation, it was necessary to severely prune this border of alyssum. It produced an attractive "mini-hedge" that was back in bloom in a matter of weeks.

marigold, which can spread quickly, reducing a 3-ft. path to a mere 12 in. (We prefer to use alyssum varieties that stay compact so that heavy pruning is not necessary. 'New Carpet of Snow' is a good choice.) This quick spreading can hamper air circulation around vegetable plants and increase the likelihood of mildew and fungus damage. If necessary, once or twice during the summer, lightly trim back these beautiful yet energetic flowers using grass clippers. Pansy borders will also need your attention. Keep them compact and blooming profusely by deadheading faded flowers and pinching back leggy stems.

The central design of your garden will be created with low-growing, compact vegetables. But your garden may not be complete without a tall tomato plant, a cucumber vine, or several berry canes. Keeping these tall varieties neatly staked or trellised will enhance the overall appearance of your kitchen garden and will prevent their fruits and vegetables from resting on the damp earth where they are susceptible to rot. Tie plants to their supports with twist ties, soft twine, or raffia. Keep the ties loose so that the stem's growth is not restricted.

HARVEST

Your kitchen garden has come full circle. You started months ago on a winter day with a piece of graph paper, a pencil, and a stack of seed catalogs. When spring arrived you nurtured tiny seedlings through unexpected cold snaps, slugs, and garden-devouring insects. Then the warm days of summer turned your fledgling garden into a beautiful flower and foliage display. And now, with autumn in sight, your hard work and patience has paid off. The abundant plants have produced a spectacular array of fruits, herbs, and vegetables.

When to harvest

The main harvest season is late summer through early autumn. However, it's possible to have something to harvest from your kitchen garden year-round.

When spring arrives, it's a sumptuous treat to dine on the first tender greens of lettuce, spinach, and chives. From this point, there will be something to pick throughout the growing season, with the majority of varieties at their prime in late summer through early autumn.

Successful winter gardening will depend on the type of plants you grow, your climate, and your ingenuity. For example, erecting cloches over lettuce and heavily mulching some root crops can extend your growing season. Frost-tolerant varieties such as leeks, kale, and rutabaga will also provide a steady stream of fresh vegetables to your table. But for the most part, your garden will rest for the winter months.

Harvest vegetables when they are at their peak of perfection. If picked too early, crops such as corn will not have developed their full flavors. If you wait too long, leafy greens can become leathery and bitter, and root crops can become hard and woody. Some vegetables need to be watched closely. A tender, young zucchini can grow into a "log" in a matter of days, and a well-formed head of broccoli can seemingly bloom overnight. Observe your garden and have fun taste testing to determine the best time to harvest each variety.

How to harvest

The kitchen gardens presented in this book are grown for their design and aesthetic appeal as well as for the vegetables they produce. Therefore, harvesting must be done thoughtfully to keep the integrity of the design flourishing as long as possible.

Your harvest will reward you with fresh-picked flavors and beautiful culinary colors.

Plants such as tomatoes, squash, peppers, strawberries, and bush beans can be harvested without disturbing the leafy parts of the plants that maintain their positions in the design. However, many vegetables, such as cabbages, cauliflower, and all root crops, require the entire plant to be pulled from the soil at harvest time, leaving large bare spots. By judiciously harvesting these crops, you can extend the life of the garden design. For example, rather than pulling up a whole group of beets in one area, harvest every other one across the entire bed. The remaining beets will carry on the design.

Tomatoes can be harvested without affecting the overall garden design.

To harvest cabbages and other root crops, you must pull the entire plant from the soil, which leaves large bare spots in your design. Judiciously harvest cabbages and other root crops to extend the life of the garden design (see the photos on the facing page).

To extend the life of the garden design, harvest every other root crop across the entire bed. For example, the top photo shows a bed of beets before harvesting. The same bed is shown below after harvesting one-third of the crop.

*Harvest just the
outer leaves of
Swiss chard so that
the inner leaves
remain to carry on
the design.*

Leafy greens such as Swiss chard, leaf lettuce, and spinach are in another harvesting category. By harvesting just the outer leaves as they mature, the young center leaves can be left to develop and maintain the pattern. This method of harvesting is particularly helpful in window boxes and container gardens. Continually removing the outer leaves keeps these small gardens from becoming overcrowded. Broccoli is also in this category. Choose broccoli varieties that tout good side-shoot production. Once you have harvested the dense, central head, leave the plant in place and enjoy its striking blue-green foliage while you continue to harvest the smaller side shoots as they appear.

If you decided to grow a succession of vegetables, replacing spring and summer varieties with fall crops, the empty spaces in your garden will be delayed even further. But as the season draws to a close and you've harvested every other onion until there is none left, and the cabbages are in their prime for making sauerkraut and coleslaw, inevitably bare spots will grow. However, your carefully designed pattern is never totally lost because the framework of paths and borders remains. In fact, the contrast between the flower borders, the mulched paths, and the geometric shapes of the dark-brown soil can be a graceful exit for your kitchen garden at season's end.

This bed of cabbages is ready for harvesting.

Although harvesting cabbages will create a bare spot, the pattern is never totally lost because the framework of paths and borders will remain.

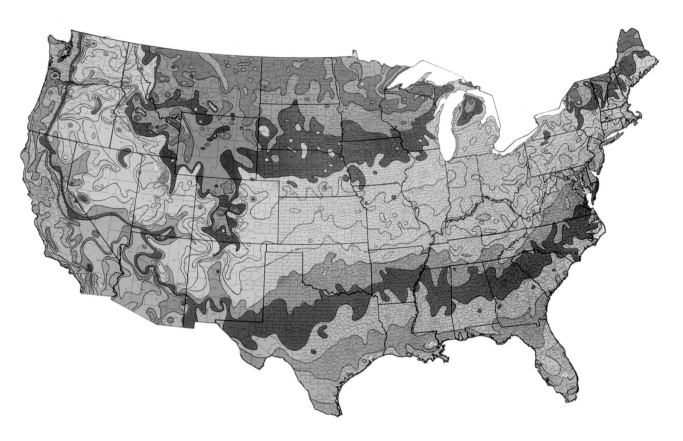

AVERAGE ANNUAL MINIMUM TEMPERATURE BY ZONE	
Zone	Temperature °F
1	below -50
2a	-45 to -50
2b	-40 to -45
3a	-35 to -40
3b	-30 to -35
4a	-25 to -30
4b	-20 to -25
5a	-15 to -20
5b	-10 to -15
6a	-5 to -10
6b	0 to -5
7a	5 to 0
7b	10 to 5
8a	15 to 10
8b	20 to 15
9a	25 to 20
9b	30 to 25
10a	35 to 30
10b	40 to 35
11	40 and above

This map shows the United States divided into 11 zones. To use the map, simply find the zone where you live and choose plants designated to grow well in your zone. Be aware, however, that other factors, including soil, exposure, moisture, and drainage, affect the growth of plants.

A variety of seeds and supplies can be found in the following catalogs. However, we categorized them according to the attributes we found most helpful about the catalog.

TOOLS AND GARDEN SUPPLIES

A. M. Leonard, Inc.
P.O. Box 816
241 Fox Dr.
Piqua, OH 45356
Phone: (800) 543-8955
Fax: (800) 433-0633
www.amleo.com

Gardener's Supply Co.
128 Intervale Rd.
Burlington, VT 05401
Phone: (800) 955-3370
www.gardenerssupply.com

Gardens Alive!
5100 Schenley Pl.
Lawrenceburg, IN 47025
Phone: (812) 537-8650
Fax: (812) 537-5108

Gurney's
Yankton, SD 57079
Phone: (605) 665-1671
Fax: (605) 665-9718

Henry Fields
415 N. Burnett
Shenandoah, IA 51602-0001
Phone: (605) 665-4491

Mellinger's, Inc.
2310 W. South Range Rd.
North Lima, OH 44452-9731
Phone: (800) 321-7444
www.mellingers.com

Natural Gardening Co.
217 San Anselmo Ave.
San Anselmo, CA 94960
Phone: (707) 766-9303
Fax: (707) 766-9747
www.naturalgardening.com

FLOWER SEEDS

J. L. Hudson, Seedsman
P.O. Box 1058
Redwood City, CA 94064

Seymour's Selected Seeds
P.O. Box 1346
Sussex, VA 23884-0346
Phone: (803) 663-3084

Thompson & Morgan, Inc.
P.O. Box 1308
Jackson, NJ 08527-0308
Phone: (800) 274-7333
www.thompson-morgan.com

HERB SEEDS

Goodwin Creek Gardens
Box 83
Williams, OR 97544
Phone: (541) 846-7357

Nichols Garden Nursery
1190 N. Pacific Highway N.E.
Albany, OR 97321-4580
Phone: (541) 928-9280
Fax: (541) 967-8406
www.pacificharbor.com/
nichols

Richters
357 Highway 47
Goodwood, Ont.
Canada L0C 1A0
Phone: (905) 640-6677
Fax: (905) 640-6641
www.richters.com

FRUITS AND BERRIES

St. Lawrence Nurseries
325 State Highway 345
Potsdam, NY 13676
Phone: (315) 265-6739

Stark Brothers Nurseries and Orchards Co.
P.O. Box 10
Louisiana, MO 63353-0010
Phone: (800) 775-6415
www.starkbros.com

VEGETABLE, FLOWER, AND HERB SEEDS

Comstock, Ferre & Co.
263 Main St.
Wethersfield, CT 06109
Phone: (860) 571-6590
Fax: (860) 571-6595

The Cook's Garden
P.O. Box 5010
Hodges, SC 29653-5010
Phone: (800) 457-9703
www.cooksgarden.com

Ferry-Morse Seeds
P.O. Box 488
Fulton, KY 42041-0488
Phone: (800) 283-6400
Fax: (800) 283-2700
www.trine.com/GardenNet/
FerryMorse

Fox Hollow Seed Co.
P.O. Box 148
McGrann, PA 16236
Phone: (724) 548-7333

Garden City Seeds
778 Highway 93 N.
Hamilton, MT 59840
Phone: (406) 961-4837

Gourmet Gardener
8650 College Blvd.
Overland Park, KS 66210
Phone: (913) 345-0490
www.gourmetgardener.com

Harris Seeds
60 Saginaw Dr.
P.O. Box 22960
Rochester, NY 14692-2960
Phone: (800) 514-4441
Fax: (716) 442-9386
www.trine.com/GardenNet/
HarrisSeeds

Johnny's Selected Seeds
Foss Hill Rd.
Albion, ME 04910-9731
Phone: (207) 437-4301
Fax: (800) 437-4290
www.johnnysselectedseeds.com

J. W. Jung Seed Co.
335 S. High St.
Randolph, WI 53957-0001
Phone: (800) 247-5864

Liberty Seed Co.
P.O. Box 806
New Philadelphia, OH 44663
Phone: (800) 541-6022
www.libertyseed.com

Otis S. Twilley Seed Co.
121 Gary Rd.
Hodges, SC 29653
Phone: (800) 622-7333

Park Seed Co., Inc.
1 Parkton Ave.
Greenwood, SC 29647-0001
Phone: (800) 845-3369
Fax: (800) 275-9941
www.parkseed.com

R. H. Shumway's
P.O. Box 1
Graniteville, SC 29829-0001
Phone: (803) 663-9771
Fax: (888) 437-2733

Seeds Blüm
HC 33 Idaho City Stage
Boise, ID 83716
Catalog, $3
Phone: (800) 528-3658
Fax: (208) 338-5658
www.seedsblum.com

Seeds of Change
P.O. Box 15700
Santa Fe, NM 87506-5700
Phone: (800) 957-3337
Fax: (888) 329-4762
www.seedsofchange.com

Shepherd's Garden Seeds
30 Irene St.
Torrington, CT 06790-6658
Phone: (860) 482-3638
Fax: (860) 482-0532
www.shepherdseeds.com

**Southern Exposure
Seed Exchange**
P.O. Box 170
Earlysville, VA 22936
Phone: (804) 973-4703
Fax: (804) 973-8717
www.southernexposure.com

Stokes
P.O. Box 548
Buffalo, NY 14240-0548
Phone: (716) 695-6980
Fax: (888) 834-3334
www.stokeseeds.com

Territorial Seed Co.
P.O. Box 157
Cottage Grove, OR 97424
Phone: (541) 942-9547
www.territorial-seed.com

Vermont Bean Seed Co.
Garden Ln.
Fair Haven, VT 05743
Phone: (803) 663-0217

W. Atlee Burpee & Co.
300 Park Ave.
Warminster, PA 18991-0001
Phone: (800) 888-1447
Fax: (800) 487-5530
www.Burpee.com

Adams, William Howard.
Nature Perfected. New York:
Abbeville Press, Inc., 1991.

Bartholomew, Mel.
Square Foot Gardening.
Emmaus, Pennsylvania: Rodale
Press, 1981.

Barton, Barbara J.
Gardening By Mail. Boston,
New York: Houghton Mifflin
Co., 1994.

Berrall, Julia S.
The Garden. New York:
The Viking Press, Inc., 1966.

**Brickel, Christopher and
Elvin McDonald, eds.**
The American Horticultural Society Encyclopedia of Gardening.
New York: Dorling Kindersley
Publishing, Inc., 1993.

**Cooke, Jean, Ann Kramer, and
Theodore Rowland-Entwistle.**
History's Timeline. New York:
Crescent Books, 1981.

Crockett, James Underwood.
Crockett's Victory Garden.
Boston: Little, Brown and Co.,
1977.

Davies, Jennifer.
The Victorian Kitchen Garden.
New York: W. W. Norton &
Co., Inc., 1988.

Hamilton, Geoff.
The Organic Garden Book.
New York: Dorling Kindersley
Publishing, Inc., 1993.

Heffernan, Maureen.
Burpee Seed Starter. New York:
MacMillan Publishing Co.,
Inc., 1997.

Hillier, Malcolm.
Malcolm Hillier's Color Garden.
New York: Dorling Kindersley
Publishing, Inc., 1995.

Hobhouse, Penelope.
Gardening Through the Ages.
New York: Simon and
Schuster, 1992.

**Hobhouse, Penelope and
Elvin McDonald, eds.**
*Gardens of the World: The Art
and Practice of Gardening.* New
York: Macmillan Publishing
Co., Inc., 1991.

Hyams, Edward.
*A History of Gardens and
Gardening.* New York: Praeger
Publishers, Inc., 1971.

Johnson, Hugh.
The Principles of Gardening.
New York: Simon and Schuster, 1979.

Jones, Louisa.
*The Art of French Vegetable
Gardening.* New York: Artisan,
1995.

Lees, Carlton B.
Gardens, Plants and Man.
Englewood Cliffs, New Jersey:
Prentice-Hall, Inc., 1970.

**Schinz, Marina and
Susan Littlefield.**
Visions of Paradise. New York:
Stewart, Tabori and Chang,
Inc., 1985.

Seymour, John.
The Self-Sufficient Gardener.
Garden City, New York:
Doubleday/Dolphin, 1980.

Splittstoesser, Walter E.
Vegetable Growing Handbook.
New York: Van Nostrand
Reinhold, 1990.

Brenzel, Kathleen Norris, ed.
Western Garden Book. Menlo
Park, California: Sunset Publishing Corporation, 1995.

Taylor, Norman, ed.
*Taylor's Encyclopedia of
Gardening.* Boston, Massachusetts: Houghton Mifflin
Co., 1948.

PUBLISHER   *Jim Childs*

ASSOCIATE PUBLISHER   *Helen Albert*

EDITORIAL ASSISTANT   *Cherilyn DeVries*

EDITOR   *Thomas McKenna*

DESIGNER/LAYOUT ARTIST   *Carol Singer*

PHOTOGRAPHER   *Michael Gertley (except where noted)*

ILLUSTRATOR   *Jan Gertley*